The Untold Story of
Kipling's American Years

CHRISTOPHER BENFEY

PENGUIN PRESS · NEW YORK
2019

PENGUIN PRESS
An imprint of Penguin Random House LLC
penguinrandomhouse.com

Copyright © 2019 by Christopher Benfey

Image credits:
Page 18: Kipling Wimpole Archive, Special Collections, University of Sussex.
35: The Minuteman, Daniel Chester French. Library of Congress, Prints and Photographs Division, LC-D416-72901.
52: MS Am 1094 (2245) f. 61, Houghton Library, Harvard University.
57: Bateman's © National Trust / Charles Thomas.
76: Felice Beato, via Wikimedia Commons.
88: Rudyard Kipling, *Just So Stories* (1912), via Wikimedia Commons.
90: Photograph by Neal Rantoul.
113: Image courtesy of Rice-Aron Library, Marlboro College, Rudyard Kipling Collection, and The Landmark Trust, USA.
134: Image courtesy of Rice-Aron Library, Marlboro College, Rudyard Kipling Collection, and The Landmark Trust, USA.
139: Clifford K. Berryman, via Wikimedia Commons.
150: *The Fog Warning*, by Winslow Homer, 1885 © Museum of Fine Arts, Boston.
167: John Lockwood Kipling (1837–1911), via Wikimedia Commons.
186: Mark Twain Papers, Bancroft Library, University of California, Berkeley.

Library of Congress Cataloging-in-Publication Data
Names: Benfey, Christopher E. G., 1954– author.
Title: If : the untold story of Kipling's American years / Christopher Benfey.
Description: New York : Penguin Press, 2019.
Identifiers: LCCN 2018058060 (print) | LCCN 2018060255 (ebook) |
ISBN 9780735221444 (ebook) | ISBN 9780735221437 (hardback)
Subjects: LCSH: Kipling, Rudyard, 1865-1936–Travel–United States. |
Authors, English–19th century–Biography. | Authors, English–20th century–Biography. |
Literature and society–United States–History–19th century. | BISAC: BIOGRAPHY & AUTOBIOGRAPHY / Literary. | HISTORY / United States / 19th Century.
Classification: LCC PR4856 (ebook) | LCC PR4856 .B39 2019 (print) |
DDC 828/.809 [B]–dc23
LC record available at https://lccn.loc.gov/2018058060

Printed in the United States of America
1 3 5 7 9 10 8 6 4 2

BOOK DESIGN BY LUCIA BERNARD

To my father

IF—

If you can keep your head when all about you
    Are losing theirs and blaming it on you,
If you can trust yourself when all men doubt you,
    But make allowance for their doubting too;
    If you can wait and not be tired by waiting,
      Or being lied about, don't deal in lies,
      Or being hated, don't give way to hating,
    And yet don't look too good, nor talk too wise:

If you can dream—and not make dreams your master;
    If you can think—and not make thoughts your aim;
    If you can meet with Triumph and Disaster
    And treat those two impostors just the same;
    If you can bear to hear the truth you've spoken
      Twisted by knaves to make a trap for fools,
    Or watch the things you gave your life to, broken,
    And stoop and build 'em up with worn-out tools:

If you can make one heap of all your winnings
    And risk it on one turn of pitch-and-toss,
    And lose, and start again at your beginnings
    And never breathe a word about your loss;
    If you can force your heart and nerve and sinew
    To serve your turn long after they are gone,
    And so hold on when there is nothing in you
    Except the Will which says to them: "Hold on!"

If you can talk with crowds and keep your virtue,
    Or walk with Kings—nor lose the common touch,
    If neither foes nor loving friends can hurt you,
    If all men count with you, but none too much;
      If you can fill the unforgiving minute
    With sixty seconds' worth of distance run,
    Yours is the Earth and everything that's in it,
    And—which is more—you'll be a Man, my son!

CONTENTS

———

PROLOGUE: THIS STRANGE EXCUSE

I.

Rudyard Kipling was born in Bombay in 1865 and educated in England. Readers have always associated this towering writer with colonial India, where he spent his early childhood and his literary apprenticeship, and with England, where he lived, in relative isolation, during the final decades of his life. Few readers are familiar with his exuberant American years, however, during the heart of the American Gilded Age. And yet Kipling wrote *The Jungle Book*, *Captains Courageous*, the first draft of *Kim*, his first "just so stories," and some of his greatest poems on the crest of a Vermont hillside overlooking the Connecticut River, with a view of Mount Monadnock "like a gigantic thumbnail pointing heavenward." A principal aim of this book is to introduce today's readers to a largely unfamiliar writer: an American Kipling.

During his astonishingly productive sojourn in New England, the key creative period in his entire career, Kipling's American accent took his English visitors by surprise. Arthur Conan Doyle brought his golf clubs to Vermont; the inventor of Sherlock Holmes taught Kipling to whack a ball around the rolling hills and shared Thanksgiving dinner with his Americanized host. Kipling announced, more than once, that he was preparing to write the Great American Novel. Among his close friends were American luminaries like Mark Twain, William James, Henry Adams, and Theodore Roosevelt. Kipling would have remained in Brattleboro, with his American wife and their two daughters, if a family quarrel—along with a pointless dispute between England and the United States over the border of Venezuela—had not cut short his New England idyll. His departure from Brattleboro in 1896, he confessed, was the hardest thing he ever had to do. "There are only two places in the world where I want to live, Bombay and Brattleboro," he said. "And I can't live in either."

A tantalizing sense of "what if" hangs over Kipling's American years, and complicates his present cultural status. His vivid creations are among the most familiar in the English language. Children all over the world are familiar with *The Jungle Book*. They thrill to Mowgli's adventures among his adoptive family of wolves or the mongoose Rikki-Tikki-Tavi's epic battles with cobras. Tales such as "How the Camel Got His Hump" and "The Elephant's Child," from Kipling's *Just So Stories*, remain beloved bedtime reading. *Kim*, Kipling's shimmering novel of international intrigue and spiritual quest, is a favorite for countless readers, young and old. And teenagers continue to be exposed to the hammering exhortations of "If—":

> If you can keep your head when all about you
> Are losing theirs and blaming it on you,
> If you can trust yourself when all men doubt you,
> But make allowance for their doubting too . . .

If you can dream—and not make dreams your master;
If you can think—and not make thoughts your aim;
If you can meet with Triumph and Disaster
And treat those two impostors just the same . . .

If you can do all these things, Kipling concludes, "Yours is the Earth and everything that's in it." A favorite of presidents and graduation speakers, of political conservatives and revolutionaries alike, "If—" was recently voted the most beloved poem in Great Britain. It is almost certainly one of the most familiar poems in the world. In 2007, Joni Mitchell released a jazz version of the poem on her album *Shine*, accompanied by Herbie Hancock on piano. It might surprise the poem's many admirers that Kipling originally used this plea for stalwart, levelheaded leadership to illustrate a story about George Washington, thus giving it an American setting. When he included it in his collected verse, he placed it opposite an elegy for his good friend Theodore Roosevelt.

From around 1890 to 1920, Rudyard Kipling was the most popular and financially successful writer in the world. At the height of his fame, in 1907, he was awarded the Nobel Prize for Literature; at forty-one, he was the youngest writer ever to win the prize and the first to write in the English language. That same year, in the company of his idol Mark Twain and the French sculptor Auguste Rodin, he was awarded an honorary degree at Oxford, to the raucous applause of an adoring crowd.

At this remove, it is difficult to recover the sheer depth of reverence once accorded Kipling. "He's more of a Shakespeare than anyone yet in this generation of ours," wrote the great American psychologist William James. His brother, the novelist Henry James, who gave the bride away at Kipling's wedding, called Kipling "the most complete man of genius" he had ever known. "Kipling's name, and Kipling's words always stir me now," Mark Twain confessed, "stir me more than do any other living man's." *The Jungle Book* was included on Sigmund Freud's list of the ten most important books in his life. The Italian Marxist Antonio Gramsci, the Argentine fabulist Jorge Luis Borges, the German poet and playwright Bertolt Brecht—they all admired Kipling, and drew inspiration from his work. When Kipling died in 1936, at the age of seventy, his ashes were buried in Poets' Corner of Westminster Abbey, alongside Shakespeare's memorial and Chaucer's grave.

New film versions of *The Jungle Book* appear regularly, seeking to displace the Disney classic of 1967, one of the most successful movies of all time. Kipling's incomparable children's books continue to be read and loved. And yet we are expected to outgrow Kipling. "It was only when I got to secondary school that I realized I wasn't supposed to like Rudyard Kipling," the historian Sir Simon Schama has written. Despite the efforts of influential admirers—including major American critics like Edmund Wilson, T. S. Eliot, Irving Howe, and Randall Jarrell—Kipling has never quite joined the ranks of unquestioned canonical writers, like Joseph Conrad and Virginia Woolf. His reputation has suffered in recent decades in particular. With the rise of postcolonial theory—a view of literature that assesses the human cost of colonial arrangements—Kipling is often treated with unease or hostility in university literature departments, as the jingoist Bard of Empire, a man on the wrong side of history. It was Kipling, after all, who wrote "The White Man's Burden," his strident plea for the United States to take up the imperial burden long held by Great Britain. And it was Kipling who wrote, notoriously, "The female of the species is more deadly than the male."

In July 2018, indignant students at the University of Manchester painted over a mural of the text of "If—," inscribed on the wall of the students' union, and replaced it with the African American writer Maya Angelou's popular 1978 poem "Still I Rise." Such actions are understandable, especially during a time when the commitments of Britain and the United States to what used to be called the Third World are increasingly in question. And yet the two poems are similar in their defiant spirit. "You may write me down in history / With your bitter twisted lies," Angelou writes, "You may trod me in the very dirt / But still, like dust, I'll rise." Kipling's poem may even have influenced "Still I Rise," for young Maya, in Angelou's *I Know Why the Caged Bird Sings*, "enjoyed and respected Kipling," and admired "If—" in particular. Gramsci, who translated "If—" into Italian, recommended it specifically for leftist revolutionaries. "Kipling's morality is imperialist only to the extent that it is closely linked to a specific historical reality," Gramsci wrote from one of Mussolini's prisons, "but there are lessons in the poem for any social group struggling for political power."

Even some of Kipling's most articulate critics have recognized the complexity of the case and the necessity to continue to read and understand his works. "*Kim* is a work of great aesthetic merit," Edward Said, one of the founding figures of postcolonial theory, proclaimed in his much-cited introduction to the novel; "it cannot be dismissed simply as the racist imagining of one fairly disturbed and ultra-reactionary imperialist." Confounding his critics, Kipling retained a deep sympathy for the despised, the marginalized, and the powerless. Kim is himself a homeless child, initially cared for by his father, a down-and-out veteran addicted to opium, and a mixed-race prostitute. Kipling's portrait of the Tibetan holy man in *Kim* is a wonder of empathy. Early tales like "Lispeth," "Without Benefit of Clergy," and "Jews in Shushan" assess the cost of racial division and bigotry. "Gunga Din" is an admiring portrait of a lowly Muslim soldier. And "The Man Who Would Be King" remains a powerful parable, as the film director John Huston recognized during the Vietnam War era, of the folly of imperial overreach. "Never trust the teller, trust the tale," as D. H. Lawrence wrote of Hawthorne, another major writer of sometimes repugnant political views.

We live in a time of rising nationalism, extreme cultural antagonism, and the breakup of empires, when the United States is as ideologically riven as it was in Kipling's time. This seems an opportune moment, following the 150th anniversary of Kipling's birth, to take a closer look at a fascinating writer and a complex historical figure. Fifty previously unknown Kipling poems were recently brought to light. A trove of lost personal documents has surfaced in Vermont, and a major exhibition on the career of Kipling's father, the prominent India-based arts administrator John Lockwood Kipling, was mounted in London and New York. Among contributions to a fuller understanding of Kipling's vagabond life, Charles Allen's account of his background in India and Sir David Gilmour's study of his political relations with the British Empire stand out. Meanwhile, contemporary Indian writers, such as Arundhati Roy and Salman Rushdie, have shown a renewed interest in this Anglo-Indian author. "No other Western writer has ever known India as Kipling knew it," Rushdie writes, "and it is this knowledge of place, and procedure, and detail that gives his stories their undeniable authority."

2.

There is one conspicuous lacuna in serious efforts to make sense of Kipling's career, however. His intense engagement with the United States—on a personal, political, and aesthetic level—has never received the sustained attention it deserves. The central focus of this book is Kipling's extraordinary American decade, extending roughly from 1889 to 1899. During the 1890s, the crucial decade for his aesthetic development, Kipling sought, deliberately and with very hard work, to turn himself into a specifically *American* writer. As a young man, he cultivated American influences like Walt Whitman and Mark Twain. A photograph of Ralph Waldo Emerson, whose essay "Self-Reliance" Kipling adopted as his personal creed, adorned his writing desk. For Kipling, America was a place of promise, of freedom, of experimentation, relatively free, in his view, from the class and caste divisions that marred England and India, a place where he could reinvent himself, as so many American writers had done before him.

If Kipling had his own sense of America, Americans developed their own version of Kipling, independent of what British or Indian readers made of him. He was the most influential writer of his time in the United States. It was largely through Kipling that naturalism, the Darwinian view that environment determines character and that only the fit survive, entered mainstream American literature. It was partly through Kipling that the cult of the strenuous life in the wild—in the jungle or the desert, among soldiers or among wolves—entered American writing.

Kipling urged his friend Theodore Roosevelt to bring this strenuous ethic into American politics; he partnered with his friend William James in conceptualizing what James called the "moral equivalent of war"—a necessary testing ground for American manhood in times of peace. And it was Kipling who introduced to the reading public the romance of the war correspondent and the international spy, those interlocking heroes of twentieth-century popular literature and film. His work profoundly influenced a generation of American writers, including Willa Cather, Stephen Crane, and Jack London (and, later, Ernest Hemingway). "There is no end of Kipling in my work," London wrote. "I would never [have] possibly written anywhere near the way I did had Kipling never been."

This book addresses key moments and encounters during the 1890s, while also offering a fresh perspective—Kipling's own—on the American Gilded Age, that fraught period first named, indelibly, by Mark Twain. It was an era, like our own, of vast disparities between rich and poor, of corruption on an appalling scale, of large-scale immigration and rampant racism, of disruptive new technologies and new media, of mushrooming factories and abandoned farms, of vanishing wildlife and the depredation of public lands. Kipling took up many of these topics in his writings. In his friend Mark Twain's view, this was not a Golden Age—that utopian dream of a perfect society in the remote past—but merely a Gilded Age, concealing the dross beneath its glittering facade.

As a historical figure in the American Gilded Age, Kipling is not just fascinating; he is unavoidable. His gravitational pull is detectable everywhere: in politics and literature, in American attitudes toward masculinity, in American preoccupations with the supernatural. In registering this gravitational pull, I have allowed myself the freedom to follow patterns of suggestion and implication wherever they lead. The opening chapters explore Kipling's relations with major American writers: Mark Twain, Henry Wadsworth Longfellow, Henry James, and others. Later chapters pursue certain strands in Kipling's life: his honeymoon in Japan, his fascination with hallucinogenic drugs, his imaginative engagement with the occult, his impact on the Spanish-American War, and the growth of the American empire. Each chapter supports a single theory: that Kipling became the writer we know, in large part, because of his deep involvement with the United States.

Kipling's influence on children's literature remains indelible. *Tarzan*, to Kipling's annoyance, was little more than an inferior remake of *The Jungle Book*; Maurice Sendak's *Where the Wild Things Are* was an inspired tribute to it. Kipling's enduring American presence is not merely literary, however. His ideas and his fictional characters have affected public policy and popular culture in ways that we do not yet fully understand. In registering Kipling's influence on American culture, I have followed him to the Washington Zoo in the company of Theodore Roosevelt, admiring the beavers and grizzly bears. I have also ventured beyond his death, mapping the surprising invocation of Kipling's writings—by ordinary soldiers and reporters, generals and movie directors, political hawks and antiwar doves—during and immediately following the Vietnam War. We cannot adequately gauge and critique Kipling's significance in American cultural and political history if we refuse to acknowledge it.

3.

Kipling's decade-long engagement with the United States can best be seen as a quest for a lost paradise. The arc of his life, as it unfolds in this book, is that of someone who discovered, when he was too young to digest the devastating news, that the world is a precarious place, and that disaster (one of the two "impostors" dismissed in "If—") can intrude at any moment. His first six years were idyllic. "My first impression is of daybreak," he wrote of his early childhood, "light and color and golden and purple fruits at the level of my shoulder." His parents were creative, supportive, artistically inclined.

Kipling's family connections were auspicious for a future writer. One of his uncles by marriage was the great Pre-Raphaelite artist Sir Edward Burne-Jones. Another was the painter Sir Edward John Poynter, president of the Royal Academy. Family friends included the visionary writer and designer William Morris and the poet Dante Gabriel Rossetti. A favorite first cousin, Stanley Baldwin, would become prime minister.

Paradise ended abruptly when five-year-old Kipling and his younger sister were farmed out, without explanation, to a sadistic foster mother in the South of England. (Intended to socialize English children born in India and shield them from disease, the practice was not uncommon.) Abandoned as a child, subject to torments both physical and psychological, he found solace in the fantasy world of books. As he matured, Kipling came to believe, as his political views veered to the right, that civilization was a veneer, keeping order over raging instincts and potential invaders. He believed in soldiers and despised comfortable people who amused themselves by "making mock of uniforms that guard you while you sleep." As George Orwell put it, Kipling "sees clearly that men can only be highly civilized while other men, inevitably less civilized, are there to guard and feed them."

Even amid his mounting fame as a writer, Kipling himself suffered so many personal disasters that nothing shook his faith in the need for dire arrangements. These views spoke in turn to American readers and writers in chaotic times, even as Kipling himself took up residence in the United States, in a sustained—and ultimately doomed—attempt to establish a safe haven for himself and for his family. Kipling once wrote that the twentieth century began in 1889. It certainly did for him. The realization that he could leave India struck him with the force of a "revelation," as he put it in his autobiography. That decisive year, he left India for good and began his nomadic years of circling the globe, in search of his destiny. And that, accordingly, is where this book begins.

4.

Many times over the past few years, I have been asked what in the world possessed me to write a book about Rudyard Kipling. The implication was that I must have had some suitable excuse for adopting such a rash, quixotic, potentially career-killing course of action. One close friend, a writer himself, warned me, again and again, that I should think twice before publishing a book on Kipling. "Don't you realize," he said, his voice rising for maximum effect, "that Kipling is *the most politically incorrect writer in the canon*?" He wondered whether I was prepared for the inevitable consequences, and suggested, darkly, that I had better have a defense in place, some sophisticated scheme of damage control, for the ensuing outrage.

I discovered soon enough that it was no use answering that I wasn't writing a defense of Kipling, and that my primary interest was historical. I wanted to map the imprint that Kipling had left on his adopted country, and the imprint that the United States had left on him. I certainly wasn't trying to *rehabilitate* him—a strange verb that I heard more than once in such conversations, as though Kipling, after years of justified imprisonment, was about to be released (by me!) upon an unsuspecting world.

Of course, it would be surprising indeed if I were the first interpreter of Kipling to be asked to defend himself. It turns out that there is even something of a tradition of such excuses. The best-known formulation comes in W. H. Auden's elegy for the Irish poet W. B. Yeats, in which he maintains that Time with a capital T "worships language and forgives / Everyone by whom it lives," adding, "Time that with this strange excuse / Pardoned Kipling and his views." Auden later excised these lines from the poem. Perhaps he had come to realize, rightly, that readers aren't called upon to pardon the views of writers they disagree with. Kipling himself was intolerant of excuses, in any case. "If—" is a plea for the self-reliant man who accepts responsibility for his actions, and an indictment of the practice of blaming others for one's failures. Time, according to Kipling, does not excuse; it is composed of one "unforgiving minute" after another.

Auden was not simply arguing that good writing will survive despite the political or religious views of the writer. He seems to be specifying, instead, that certain writers, among whom he numbers Yeats and Kipling, are part of the lifeblood of language itself. These writers aren't merely embedded in our language, Auden suggests; our language lives through them and by them. Auden's claim seems particularly apt for Kipling, who is said to have bequeathed more familiar quotations to the English language (from "East is East and West is West" to "That's another story") than any other writer since Shakespeare. According to Orwell, "Kipling is the only English writer of our time who has added phrases to the language."

Ultimately, it is Kipling's complexity, as a writer and a historical figure—especially in his relations with the United States—that I hope to convey in this book. Borges was impatient with those who reduced Kipling's thirty-five volumes to a "mere apologist" for empire. "What is indisputable is that Kipling's prose and poetic works are infinitely more complex than the theses they elucidate," he wrote in a review of 1941. "Like all men, Rudyard Kipling was many men (English gentleman, Eurasian journalist, bibliophile, spokesman for soldiers and mountains), but none with more conviction than the artificer."

Kipling at his uncanny best offers little of the pat solutions, the ringing advice that he is often reputed to supply. Even his declamatory "If—" hangs on one of the oddest, one of the *iffiest,* words in the English language. Instead, he draws us, word by slippery word, to the very brink, to the ultimate mysteries of language and life. And those mysteries, he leads us to believe, lie somewhere in the specific *interlocking* of our words and our worlds—our lived experience. Our initials, our given names, our mother tongues, our verbal slips, our hasty ensuing excuses: how strange these are, Kipling tells us in tale after tale, how internal to who we are.

Perhaps the most eloquent recent plea for readers to give Kipling a fresh look, despite his conspicuous liabilities and limitations, comes from Michael Ondaatje in *The English Patient.* As the Canadian nurse Hana reads *Kim* aloud to the mysterious patient, whose true identity is as enigmatic as Kim's own, he gives her a reading lesson. *Kim* must be read slowly, he tells her, to appreciate Kipling's rhythms, his sinuous sentence-sounds. "Watch carefully where the commas fall so you can discover the natural pauses," he instructs her. And when Kip, the Punjabi mine detector, all too aware of the historical disaster of British colonialism in India, appears in the abandoned villa, he is said to come directly from the pages of *Kim,* as his nickname, an amalgam of Kipling and Kim, suggests. "As if," writes Ondaatje, "the pages of Kipling had been rubbed in the night like a magic lamp. A drug of wonders." Ondaatje implies that there is still potential magic to be found in Kipling's books, if we only know where to look.

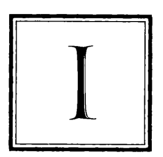

Chapter One

—

A DENIZEN OF THE MOON

I.

It was a hot and dusty afternoon in the middle of August 1889. Mark
Twain was sequestered from a prying public in his summer refuge in
Elmira, New York, correcting the proofs of *A Connecticut Yankee in King
Arthur's Court.* In his darkening mood at the time, Twain was convinced
that this dystopian novel laced with violence would be his last. There
was a hesitant knock at the door. His oldest daughter, Susy, showed in,
unannounced, a short, bespectacled young man of twenty-three. The
stranger had bristling eyebrows, an odd accent, and an even more peculiar name. Presenting his card, he introduced himself as Rudyard
Kipling, a reporter for the Allahabad *Pioneer,* in remotest India, and conveyed his intense admiration for Twain's books. Under ordinary circumstances, Twain, after a few minutes of friendly banter, would have shown
the intruder the door, but there was something about the visitor's

command of language that mesmerized him—"talk which might be likened to footprints," Twain remarked later, "so strong and definite was the impression which it left behind."

Mark Twain had made it his business to be difficult to find, but Kipling was a newspaper reporter, trained to get the story. Later, he summarized his loopy itinerary in quest of his hero: "They said in Buffalo that he was in Hartford, Connecticut; and again they said 'perchance he is gone upon a journey to Portland'; and a big, fat drummer [a traveling salesman] vowed that he knew the great man intimately, and that Mark was spending the summer in Europe." Kipling was so confused that he boarded the wrong train, only to be "incontinently turned out by the conductor three-quarters of a mile from the station, amid the wilderness of railway tracks." Discouraged, Kipling returned on foot, battered suitcase in one hand and overcoat in the other, to the Buffalo train station, where he learned from a stranger the name of his true destination: "Elmira is the place. Elmira in the State of New York—this state, not two hundred miles away." Around midnight, Kipling checked himself into a "frowzy" hotel in Elmira, only to be told, yet again, that he might have made the journey for nothing. "Yes, they knew all about 'that man Clemens,' but reckoned he was not in town; had gone East somewhere."

And so it was that, after a sleepless night, the feverish quest for Twain's whereabouts resumed at dawn—"Morning revealed Elmira," as Kipling wrote—in a rented carriage in a small industrial city, its main streets washed clean by the recent flooding of the Chemung River. After a few more dead ends, Kipling's driver finally pulled up at a "miserable, little, white wood shanty," where he was met by a young woman sketching thistles and goldenrod. The artist, who turned out to be Susy Clemens, quickly "set the pilgrimage on the right path," directing him to a pretty house a little further on—the home of Mark Twain's brother-in-law. And there, finally, Kipling met "this man I had learned to love and admire fourteen thousand miles away."

As the two men talked, Twain was astonished by the breadth of his young visitor's knowledge. "I believed that he knew more than any person I had met before," he wrote admiringly. How exactly did the outlandish name, the exotic accent, and the job on the Indian newspaper come together, he wondered. And what in the world was this Rudyard Kipling doing in Elmira, of all places? They sat on the veranda while Kipling caught his breath and regaled Twain and his daughter with his extraordinary talk of faraway lands. Transfixed by this traveler from "a land made out of poetry and moonlight," Susy felt that she was listening to "a denizen of the moon."

2.

How did this lunar visitor appear to his American hosts? His odd first name was easily explained. His father, John Lockwood Kipling, was trained as a sculptor and potter, and employed at the Staffordshire Potteries around present-day Stoke-on-Trent. His mother, Alice, was visiting her brother in the neighborhood, and joined a holiday party for a picnic at Lake Rudyard. It was there that Kipling's parents met and fell in love, and they commemorated the occasion when they named their first child Joseph Rudyard Kipling. The American Civil War, which figured so prominently in Twain's life, also had a bearing on Kipling's early years. The naval blockade of the Confederacy prevented Southern cotton from reaching England, opening markets to Indian cotton instead. In 1865, the last year of the war, Lockwood and Alice, pregnant with their first child, moved to Bombay, flush with the cotton trade, where Lockwood took a job teaching art and design at a newly founded school.

It was in England, where Kipling and his younger sister, Trix, were farmed out to a harsh foster family, that Kipling first discovered the world of books. His father sent him *Robinson Crusoe* and the Brothers Grimm,

Rudyard Kipling and his father in India, c. 1883.

without realizing that his miserable son was living a fairy tale, part "Hansel and Gretel" and part "Little Red Riding Hood." Four years at a second-rate private school, mainly for the children of military officers, followed. Diminutive, dark-skinned, bespectacled, Kipling was an exotic figure to his classmates; he shocked his teachers by announcing that his favorite poet was the disreputable Walt Whitman. To Kipling and his friends, America—the land of Tom Sawyer and Uncle Remus—seemed a place of mischief and boyish high spirits. Too poor for college, Kipling returned to India for a job with a local newspaper in Lahore, the northern outpost now in Pakistan, where his father had become director of the art school and museum.

During what he called his "seven years hard" as a newspaper reporter in northern India, Kipling remade himself as a tough-minded observer of the life of ordinary soldiers. He followed British troops on their sometimes dangerous missions along the Afghan border and watched, with an eagle eye, the behavior of the British colonial community at work and at play. Soon he began publishing short stories and poems based on these experiences, garnering a local readership for his racy accounts of local life, in a pulp series for travelers called the Indian Railway Library. In 1889, seeking a broader scope for his work, Kipling began his epic journey around the world and gradually transformed himself into an international writer. He traveled to Hong Kong and Japan. Most importantly, he traveled to the United States, where his dream of restoring something of the wondrous early life he had led as a child, in Bombay, took hold. Part of that dream was to meet Mark Twain.

3.

Kipling's pilgrimage to Elmira had begun two months earlier with an unexpected thump. Just short of the dock in San Francisco Bay, the American steamer he had boarded in Yokohama, the *City of Peking*, had run aground in a mudbank. Already exhausted from a violent storm at sea, the exasperated passengers were ferried the rest of the way in a pitching tugboat. Over the previous few days, tensions on board had erupted between American and British passengers, and Kipling had grown tired of Americans bragging about the wonders of their can-do country. "When the *City of Peking* steamed through the Golden Gate," he wrote belligerently, "I saw with great joy that the block-house which guarded the mouth of the 'finest harbor in the world, Sir,' could be silenced by two gunboats from Hong Kong with safety, comfort, and dispatch." He felt disoriented in the strange city. Glancing at the hotel register, and misreading the word "India," a local reporter asked him what he thought of Indiana. Kipling made his way to the offices of the

San Francisco Call, eager to question the staff about the magazine's most famous writer, Sam Clemens, who had served his apprenticeship there twenty-five years earlier, and who had adopted the pen name Mark Twain as he began his own conquest of America.

To travel to London from Bombay, a route via Japan and the United States is not self-evident. The western route, up through the Suez Canal, open since 1869, and into the Mediterranean, is far shorter (some four thousand miles versus more like eighteen thousand). Kipling decided to go the eastern route on impulse. His closest friends, Alexander and Edmonia Hill, of Allahabad, were also heading for London, but for them the Pacific detour made sense. Edmonia, known to her friends as "Ted," was an American, the daughter of the president of Beaver College, in rural Pennsylvania. Her husband, a kindly Ulster-born professor of science, was a passionate photographer and relished some exotic sightseeing in Rangoon, Hong Kong, and Japan.

It was almost a family outing for the three globe-trotters. The childless Hills had all but adopted Rudyard Kipling. He rented a room in their house; he adored Ted Hill, tall and elegant and seven years his senior. He later set one of his finest children's stories, "Rikki-Tikki-Tavi," a self-portrait as adopted mongoose (Rikki = RK), in the Hills' bungalow. In San Francisco, the professor and his wife departed for Pennsylvania, where Kipling, who had contracted for a series of travel letters to be published in the Allahabad *Pioneer*, planned to meet them in a couple of months. The traditional journey across America, for Dickens and other European travelers, began with the crowded cities of the East and found release in the great open spaces of the western plains and the sublimity of the Rocky Mountains. Kipling planned to start in the West instead, where Mark Twain had begun his career, and then make his way gradually, over three thousand miles of rivers, mountains, and prairies, toward what the great man derisively called, in *The Adventures of Huckleberry Finn*, "sivilization." Kipling's ragged pilgrimage to Elmira would last two and a half months, and extend across the entire length of the North American continent—"From Sea to Sea," as he titled his published letters.

From Twain's fellow San Francisco bohemian Bret Harte, chronicler of the hardscrabble gold rush towns, Kipling took his epigraph for his American letters: "Serene, indifferent to fate, Thou sittest at the western gate." A New York native who had moved to California at seventeen, Harte had almost single-handedly revitalized the American short story, bringing earthy dialect and lowlife characters into such wildly popular tales as "The Luck of Roaring Camp" and "The Outcasts of Poker Flat." Like Twain before him, who learned all that he could from Harte's pioneering western tales, Kipling had been studying Harte as a model for his own stories, about the British in India. "Why buy Bret Harte," Kipling had asked his editor at the *Pioneer*, "when I was prepared to supply home-grown fiction on the hoof?"

From Twain, Kipling adopted a voice for his travel writing—ironic, hyperbolic, but capable of emotional highs and lows. The journey was also an apprenticeship. This citizen of Anglo-India, a country unto itself, as Kipling conceived of it in *Plain Tales from the Hills*, was intensely curious about the United States. Both countries, as he saw them, were colonial regimes ruled by an "Anglo-Saxon" elite, and peopled by indigenous inhabitants—"East Indians" in one case, "Red Indians" in the other—in need of discipline, uplift, and administrative leadership. At the same time, he was appalled by American attitudes toward Native Americans. "Some of the men I meet have a notion that we in India are exterminating the native in the same fashion," he wrote indignantly.

All across the rugged country, Kipling saw parallels between the two lands. Wasn't arid Arizona a bit like Afghanistan? And didn't Chicago, teeming with its "more than a million people," stand on "the same sort of soil as Calcutta?" As he traveled, Kipling heard a great deal about American "versatility," but he remained skeptical. A man, he felt, "must serve an apprenticeship to one craft and learn that craft all the days of his life if he wishes to excel therein." His own craft was writing, and he was learning all he could from the American masters, Bret Harte and Mark Twain, above all.

4.

Kipling began his dispatches from America—described by Mark Twain as "dashing, free-handed, brilliant letters"—on a high, almost manic pitch, as though he was afraid the continent might not supply him with sufficiently vibrant material. "San Francisco is a mad city," he wrote, "inhabited for the most part by perfectly insane people whose women are of a remarkable beauty." The insanity extended to the unmarked streets, as Kipling found himself "tangled . . . up in a hopeless maze of small wooden houses, dust, street-refuse, and children who play with empty kerosene tins." The vast Palace Hotel where he stayed was another inscrutable maze, "a seven-storied warren of humanity with a thousand rooms in it."

Most terrifying of all was Chinatown. Almost the first thing that Kipling had witnessed in San Francisco, on his first walk through town, was a Chinese man "who had been stabbed in the eye and was bleeding like a pig." And so it was with some trepidation, and much verbal heightening, that he ventured into a Chinese house of ill repute, and began to explore the "brick-walled and wooden-beamed subterranean galleries, strengthened with iron-framed doors and gates." As he burrowed down through the levels belowground, he crawled past Chinese men "in bunks, opium-smokers, brothels, and gambling hells, till I had reached the second cellar—was, in fact, in the labyrinths of a warren."

Kipling was led downstairs to yet another cellar, unbearably hot, where a game of poker was in full swing. The men at the table were in "semi-European dress," pigtails curled under their hats; one looked Eurasian, according to Kipling, and turned out on closer inspection to be Mexican. The ghostly scene Kipling describes is dreamlike, uncanny, retrieved, literally and figuratively, from the depths. "We were all deep down under the earth," he wrote, "and save for the rustle of a blue gown sleeve and the ghostly whisper of the cards as they were shuffled and played, there was no sound." An argument broke out between the Mexican player and one of the Chinese men. Suddenly a shot rang out. Kipling dove to the floor amid a whirl of smoke. The Mexican had disappeared. "Still gripping the table, the Chinaman said: 'Ah!' in the tone that a man would use when, looking up from his work suddenly, he sees a well-known friend in the doorway." Then he collapsed to the floor, shot through the stomach. Worried that the Chinese card players might mistake him for the murderous Mexican, Kipling, panic-stricken, fled the scene of the crime. "I found the doorway and, my legs trembling under me, reached the protection of the clear cool night, the fog, and the rain."

It is all beautifully done, this little anecdote of exotic depravity belowground. And yet the poker game gone awry seems suspiciously close, in setting and narrative detail, to Bret Harte's popular poem "The Heathen Chinee." We know that Kipling particularly admired the poem, and so did Mark Twain, who collaborated with Harte on a play based on it. Originally titled "Plain Language from Truthful James," Harte's poem is about a cardsharp named Nye who is outfoxed by a Chinese gambler named, suggestively, Ah Sin. (Kipling's Chinese card player, with the blue gown sleeve, says just one word, "Ah.") Pretending barely to understand the rules of poker, Ah Sin plays the same card that Nye has just drawn from his sleeve. It turns out that Ah Sin is hiding twenty-four cards in his own long sleeves, "which was coming it strong."

5.

Mark Twain was on Kipling's mind as he ventured up the coast into the Pacific Northwest, hoping to do some leisurely fishing before heading eastward to Chicago. "All I remember is a delightful feeling that Mark Twain's Huckleberry Finn and Mississippi Pilot were quite true," he wrote of a journey by steamboat on the Columbia River, "and that I could almost recognize the very reaches down which Huck and Jim had drifted." No sooner was the dreamy mood established, however, than it was shattered by the grisly sounds of a salmon lift and a cannery. "At the next bend we sighted a wheel—an infernal arrangement of wire-gauze compartments worked by the current and moved out from a barge in shore to scoop up the salmon as he races up the river." Into the jaws of the cannery they went, a thousand salmon, to be gutted, beheaded, and de-tailed, cut into chunks, and soldered into cans, all at the hands of ghostly Chinese workers, whose nimble fingers were integral parts of the mechanized butchery. "Inside, on a floor ninety by forty, the most civilized and murderous of machinery," he wrote. "Outside, three foot-steps, the thick-growing pines and the immense solitude of the hills."

After his Huck Finn adventures on the Columbia River, Kipling returned to San Francisco to begin his long railroad journey eastward. He crossed the Rockies on train trestles that sometimes reached almost three hundred feet into the air. Stopping in Salt Lake City, he snarkily described the Mormon women as so ugly that polygamy must be "a blessed institution." Turning northward, he made a stopover in Yellow-stone, on the Fourth of July, to admire the geysers and "tourist-trampled" hot springs—"greenish grey hot water, and here and there pit-holes dry as a rifled tomb in India."

Among the throng at Old Faithful, he met a "very trim maiden" from New Hampshire who seemed to have "just stepped out of one of Mr. James's novels"—presumably Henry James's popular novella *Daisy Miller.* She proceeded to lecture Kipling "on American literature, the nature and inwardness of Washington society, the precise value of Cable's works as compared with 'Uncle Remus' Harris, and a few other things that had nothing whatever to do with geysers, but were altogether delightful." Aside from his growing admiration for American women, Kipling is inviting us into his own literary workshop here. For he himself was assiduously studying the work of the New Orleans local-color writer George

Washington Cable, Mark Twain's lecture partner during their "Twins of Genius" tour of 1884, and the Uncle Remus tales of Joel Chandler Harris. Both Cable and Harris were centrally concerned with bringing African American voices into their work, as of course was Mark Twain, with sometimes unfortunate results. While Kipling seems barely to have noticed African Americans during his journey, he did increasingly register the complex origins of the American people.

As he rode trains and spent nights in hotels, Kipling was impressed with the Americans he met. Adopting the celebratory tone of Walt Whitman, he predicted greatness for this raw and diverse populace, destined to be "the biggest, finest, and best people on the surface of the globe." The "Man of the Future," he proclaimed, would be "the Anglo-American-German-Jew," with "just the least little kink in his hair now and again; he'll carry the English lungs above the Teuton feet that can walk for ever; and he will wave long, thin, bony Yankee hands with the big blue veins on the wrist, from one end of the earth to the other." This ethnically amalgamated American would excel in more than physical prowess. "He'll be the finest writer, poet, and dramatist, 'specially dramatist, that the world as it recollects itself has ever seen. By virtue of his Jew blood—just a little, little drop—he'll be a musician and a painter too," Kipling predicted. "There is nothing known to man that he will not be, and his country will sway the world with one foot as a man tilts a see-saw plank!" Amid the stereotypes, Kipling is imagining himself, with his own culturally hybrid background, taking part in the great American melting pot of poets and painters.

For mechanized killing on a gigantic scale, the salmon cannery on the Columbia River proved to be nothing in comparison to the butchery of pigs and cattle that Kipling witnessed in the slaughterhouses of Chicago, another popular tourist destination. The "railway of death" was how Kipling described the unknowing cattle led to slaughter by a designated red Texan steer, the "Judas" of the herd. He watched in horror as this "red devil" enticed one unwitting cow after another. "I saw his broad back jogging in advance of them, up a lime-washed incline where I was forbidden to follow. Then a door shut, and in a minute back came Judas with the air of a virtuous plough-bullock and took up his place in his byre. Somebody laughed across the yard, but I heard no sound of cattle from the big brick building into which the mob had disappeared."

Even women came to watch the butchery, Kipling noted, "as they would come to see the slaughter of men." He examined the women instead, and one woman in particular.

> And there entered that vermilion hall a young woman of large mold, with brilliantly scarlet lips, and heavy eyebrows, and dark hair that came in a "widow's peak" on the forehead. She was well and healthy and alive, and she was dressed in flaming red and black, and her feet (know you that the feet of American women are like unto the feet of fairies?) her feet, I say, were cased in red leather shoes. She stood in a patch of sunlight, the red blood under her shoes, the vivid carcasses stacked round her, a bullock bleeding its life away not six feet away from her, and the death factory roaring all round her. She looked curiously, with hard, bold eyes, and was not ashamed.

This painterly study in scarlet is an unsettling mixture of attraction and repulsion.

6.

Kipling was able to make a closer study of American women when he arrived in Beaver, Pennsylvania—renamed Musquash ("muskrat") in *From Sea to Sea*—to stay with Ted Hill's family for a couple of idle months. Her father was the president of the Beaver College for Women, a strict

Methodist institution, located in a town where dancing and alcohol of any kind were strictly prohibited. "One heard a good deal of this same dread of drink in Musquash," Kipling noted, "and even the maidens seemed to know too much about its effects upon certain unregenerate youths"—youths much like himself, presumably. Kipling was mesmerized by the maidens, who seemed, despite prohibitions of various kinds, to be far worldlier than their English counterparts. They seemed to have stepped from the pages of *Little Women*. "I had the honor of meeting in the flesh, even as Miss Louisa Alcott drew them, Meg and Jo and Beth and Amy, whom you ought to know," he informed his readers back home.

Kipling ventured an explanation, gleaned from his reading of Henry James, for their forthright manner. "From her fifteenth year the American maiden moves among 'the boys' as a sister among brothers," he wrote.

> As to the maiden, she is taught to respect herself, that her fate is in her own hands, and that she is the more stringently bound by the very measure of the liberty so freely accorded to her. Wherefore, in her own language, "she has a lovely time" with about two or three hundred boys who have sisters of their own. . . . And so time goes till the maiden knows the other side of the house,— knows that a man is not a demi-god nor a mysteriously veiled monster, but an average, egotistical, vain, gluttonous, but on the whole companionable, sort of person, to be soothed, fed, and managed—knowledge that does not come to her sister in England till after a few years of matrimony. And then she makes her choice.

The whole run of sentences about sisters and self-respect reveals something of Kipling's emotional life as a young man. For Kipling, it is reasonable to say, had already made *his* choice during those lazy days in Beaver, at least as far as choosing to marry an American maiden. Ted

Hill had been Kipling's ideal woman for a long time. American maidens were more like sisters than lovers, as he saw it. He promptly managed to fall in love with Ted Hill's younger sister Caroline and succeeded in extracting from her an informal understanding that he was her choice, too, and that she would eventually join him in England. Such falling in love with sisters would remain the strange and puzzling hallmark of Kipling's romantic life. He seemed haunted, in particular, by the fear that he might choose *the wrong sister,* a theme he had explored in his superb early story "False Dawn," in which a British officer, at a twilight party further darkened by a dust storm, mistakenly proposes to the wrong sister.

7.

The major destination of Kipling's American pilgrimage was not Beaver, Pennsylvania, however. It was Elmira, New York, where he suddenly found himself, that hot August morning, face-to-face with the greatest living American writer of all. "What had I come to do or say?" Kipling asked himself, trying to get his bearings, and struggling to register the sheer momentousness of the encounter. "A big, darkened drawing-room; a huge chair; a man with eyes, a mane of grizzled hair, a brown mustache covering a mouth as delicate as a woman's, a strong, square hand shaking mine, and the slowest, calmest, levellest voice in all the world saying, 'Well, you think you owe me something, and you've come to tell me so. That's what I call squaring a debt handsomely.'"

Kipling had to jog himself to listen to what "the oracle" was saying, with "the long, slow surge of the drawl." International copyright was the first topic, the pirating of American works in England and vice versa. "What I saw with the greatest clearness," Kipling wrote, "was Mark Twain being forced to fight for the simple proposition that a man has as much right to the work of his brains (think of the heresy of it!) as to the labor of his hands. When the old lion roars, the young whelps growl." The two writers—the lion known the world over and the whelp, for the moment at least, completely unknown—spoke for two hours. Kipling asked if a sequel to *The Adventures of Tom Sawyer* might be hoped for, with Tom grown up and married to Becky Thatcher. Twain joked that he might write the sequel in two ways. "In one I would make him rise to great honor and go to Congress, and in the other I should hang him. Then the friends and enemies of the book could take their choice." And now it was Kipling who argued, mildly, and in seeming contradiction to the discussion of copyright, that Tom Sawyer belonged to his readers, "was real," and wasn't Mark Twain's property anymore. "He belongs to us."

The conversation turned to autobiography. Twain had published reminiscences of his childhood and youth, such as his magnificent "Old Times on the Mississippi," which appeared in *The Atlantic* in 1875. Twain described his apprenticeship as a riverboat pilot until the Civil War and the railroads put an end to the great age of steamboats. He had accumulated many false starts on a full-scale autobiography in the years since. By 1885, four years before Kipling's visit, he had begun experimenting with dictation as a means to release his buried memories, but he was disappointed with the results. "It is not in human nature to write the truth about itself," Twain told Kipling. As the meeting at Elmira drew to a close, Kipling remembered all the things that he had forgotten to ask Mark Twain. For Twain, too, the encounter was too short. He and Susy, he felt, were like "Eric Ericsons who had discovered a continent but did not suspect the horizonless extent of it." Kipling "was a stranger to me, and to all the world," he wrote, "and remained so for twelve months; then he became suddenly known, and universally known."

But the big thing, the important thing, was this: Rudyard Kipling, unknown newspaper reporter, had successfully tracked down Mark Twain. "The landing of a twelve-pound salmon was nothing to it," he

Chapter Two

——

AT LONGFELLOW'S GRAVE

I.

As Kipling's American journey drew to an end, everything reminded him of home. From Elmira, he zigzagged south for a very hot visit to Washington, D.C. "Simla-ish" was how the city's wide avenues and "the refined look of the people on the streets" struck Kipling, reminding him of Simla, the summer refuge, in the foothills of the Himalayas, of the British colonial elite. Having covered the military in India, Kipling was curious about its American counterpart. Poking around army headquarters, he met a cavalry officer with a special interest in the Native Americans of Arizona and New Mexico. When Kipling mentioned the folklore of India, a favorite subject of his father's, he was surprised to learn that the officer had corresponded with ethnological experts in India. During a brief stopover in Philadelphia, he found three Parsis staying at his hotel; another Indian in their party had studied at Lockwood Kipling's Bombay art school. All knew the name Kipling.

Two days later, Kipling was in New York, tracking down, at his father's insistence, the artist Lockwood de Forest, who worked with the Tiffany decorating firm. De Forest had traveled to India in 1881 and met the other Lockwood, Kipling's father; the two men had set up an export business in teak furniture carved by native craftsmen. Kipling was astonished by de Forest's East Tenth Street house, with its flamboyant teak entryway based on an Indian prototype, "one of the very luxurioustest houses I've ever seen." De Forest urged Kipling to visit Joseph Henry Harper, head of the Harper and Brothers firm, before leaving New York. The visit did not go well. "Young man," Harper reportedly said, "this house is devoted to the production of literature." It was a bitter reminder that the success Kipling had achieved in India might not translate so easily into a big career in the United States or in England.

The same day, after "searchings manifold," Kipling visited his "long lost uncle," Henry Macdonald, the black sheep of his mother's siblings, at his Wall Street office. Everything had seemed in place for Uncle Harry—an Oxford degree, close friendships with the artists Edward Burne-Jones and William Morris, a future position in the Indian Civil Service, a fiancée—when he bailed out at the last moment and fled, alone and without explanation, to New York. It took him a year to find work, in the lowly position of proofreader for *The New York Times*. Later, he was employed by a stock brokerage. "It was a queer meeting," Kipling wrote, "for we had to talk family affairs for an hour with the ticker reeling off the prices of stock in our ear." Time had "not dealt kindly" with Uncle Harry, Kipling noted, a warning that not all daring schemes turned out well. "I talked to a man who hasn't seen my mother for 30 years and horrible sensations of age crept over me," Kipling wrote uneasily, eager to leave New York behind.

2.

A violent storm barreled into coastal New England just as Kipling prepared to leave for Boston, the site of his final literary pilgrimage. It was the "first big equinoctial" of the season, he was told, and its full force struck as he made his way through the flooded streets of New York, in which sewage and seawater were "mingling cheerfully in the washed out bar rooms underground." Kipling had booked a leisurely steamer, but rough seas forced him to take the train instead, where passengers arrived "with awful stories of hotels knocked down, houses ripped open and breakwaters turned down by the Sea."

The storm was still at full strength when Kipling's train pulled into Boston, his tempestuous mood a strange amalgam of anxiety and exultation. "I trembled for the pear trees when I heard it howling among the chimneys of Boston," he wrote, "and went down to the wharves and saw the battered and strained tramps of the sea sneak into the harbor." He meant tramp steamers, merchant ships without a fixed schedule. "Yet somehow," he added, "I caught myself wishing that I had been out in it." Along with his enthusiastic, faintly suicidal wish to be "out in it," Kipling felt a sudden inspiration to write poetry. He had brought along a notebook to safeguard his "rough attempts," as the danger of the stormy seas and the impulse to write verse churned together in his mind.

The storm-tossed journey had taken a physical toll on Kipling. He spent the first day and a half confined in his Boston hotel, too sick to explore the city. "Carry me home in a coffin," he joked. By September 13 (ominously, a Friday), he was feeling sturdy enough to embark on some gentle sightseeing. For his first destination, he headed straight to a graveyard: "Well, this morn I got up and in what was left of the gale paid a pilgrimage to the tomb of Longfellow." As he walked among the picturesque hills and majestic trees of Mount Auburn Cemetery, on the outskirts of Cambridge, Kipling was overwhelmed by a dark mood, "an attack of 'blues,'" as he called it, "insomuch that I could have knocked out my brains against the nearest vault." He lingered to make a sketch of Longfellow's tomb. Returning to Cambridge, he stopped at the poet's stately Georgian house on Brattle Street, with a view down to the Charles River, to pay his respects.

Kipling's inner weather continued to fluctuate with the waning storm. Increasingly, he felt himself on the verge of something momentous. He detected the stirrings of literary imagination. And he was experiencing other emotions as well. "I am writing this in the back room of a druggist's store in Wellesley while I wait for my train," Kipling wrote Ted Hill. He had gone to Wellesley, just west of Boston, in mid-September to visit the famous women's college where Caroline Taylor, whom he was hoping to marry, was enrolled as a special student. Kipling barely knew Caroline, who was religiously devout, unlike him, and who knew little of the world beyond Beaver, Pennsylvania. That she was Ted Hill's younger sister seemed sufficient allure. Their tenuous relationship would only last a few more weeks. In the college's dining hall, Kipling felt conspicuously exposed: "the one man among four hundred girls—and they all looked at me—looked at me good."

3.

Four days later, Kipling traveled west to nearby Concord, the home of many of the American writers he most admired. Concord was also the site of the first major battlefield of the American Revolution. "This day has more impressed me with the 'might majesty dominion and power' of the Great American Nation than any other," he told Hill, quoting from the Anglican prayer book. As he stood in front of Daniel Chester French's famous statue of an American rebel, one hand on the plough where he has left his coat, while the other resolutely holds his flintlock rifle—a man visibly leaving one way of life for another, more daring one, and at a minute's notice—Kipling was once again assailed by a complex mood that he found difficult to describe. He came "very near to choking," he confessed, as he contemplated the minuteman, realizing that he himself was "standing on the first battlefield in the very beginning of things." What did it all mean? Kipling hardly knew. "Not even the sight of Hawthorne's manse, nor his grave nor Emerson's nor even Louisa M. Alcott's touched me half so much. And I wonder why."

Much was at play for Kipling as he contemplated the statue of the minuteman: a future new life with an American wife, replacing his roving bachelor's existence; a closer relation to the United States, with its rich history of independence and its inspiring writers, in whose

Daniel Chester French's statue, the Minuteman.

company he hoped to assume an honored place; a shifting, vertiginous sense of just who he himself was amid the gale. Again he felt the impulse *to write*. "My spare moments (they are not many) have been taken up by a Literary Scheme which when settled in my mind I will unfold to you," he promised Ted Hill. He dropped two clues concerning the nature of the mysterious scheme. First, there was the minuteman statue itself, commemorating "the very beginning of things." Second, there was Kipling's silent vigil at Longfellow's grave.

Why then was Longfellow so insistently on Kipling's mind that a pilgrimage to the poet's grave was the first order of business when he felt well enough to walk? A deep personal connection was at work, along with that pressing sense of inspiration. For if there was a poet in Kipling's American Parnassus to match Mark Twain in prose, it was Henry Wadsworth Longfellow, whose wide-ranging poems—from nostalgic evocations of growing up in a village on the Maine shore to racy ballads of roving pirates on the Spanish Main—were wildly popular in England and British India. Kipling was hardly alone in placing Longfellow first among American poets. During much of the nineteenth century, before his poems came to seem old-fashioned in comparison with Whitman's or Emily Dickinson's, Longfellow's preeminence was unquestioned. He was the author of national epics like "The Song of Hiawatha" and "Evangeline." Every schoolchild knew "Paul Revere's Ride" and "The Village Blacksmith." Longfellow's translation of Dante's *Divine Comedy* was the standard version in English. His antislavery poems were influential in the fight for abolition.

But Kipling admired Longfellow for three things in particular. First, Longfellow's appeal to a broad range of readers was something that Kipling sought to emulate from the start. Second, Kipling followed Longfellow in repurposing inherited forms like the ballad. One of the first poems that Kipling was drawn to, when he tried his hand at writing verses as a schoolboy, was the seductive meter of "Hiawatha," which, as he noted wryly in *Something of Myself,* "saved all the bother about rhyme." And third, Longfellow was an emphatically cosmopolitan writer, bringing all sorts of national traditions—Italian, Spanish, German, Scandinavian, and even Native American—into his work. Longfellow was a world poet in ways that Bombay-born Kipling aspired to. All three of these literary commitments—to wide popularity, to popular forms, and to diverse national traditions—were mutually reinforcing.

With its multiple debts to other poets and poetic traditions, Longfellow's poetry was a sophisticated echo chamber. One poem in particular was on Kipling's mind as he wandered the Boston streets and looked out on the ships in the harbor. This was "My Lost Youth," one of Longfellow's most loved poems, which recalls his childhood in Portland, Maine.

> Often I think of the beautiful town
> That is seated by the sea;
> Often in thought go up and down
> The pleasant streets of that dear old town,
> And my youth comes back to me.
> And a verse of a Lapland song
> Is haunting my memory still:
> "A boy's will is the wind's will,
> And the thoughts of youth are long, long thoughts."

The refrain, which gave the title to Robert Frost's first book of poems, *A Boy's Will,* comes from an Icelandic poem translated into German by the eighteenth-century writer Johann Gottfried Herder, and then translated from German into English by Longfellow. During the ensuing months, Kipling worked on a story based on the Indian theme of metempsychosis, or the transmigration of souls, while specifically engaging both the themes of Longfellow's poetry and its very nature as a reverberating echo chamber.

4.

One of Kipling's most admired stories, "The Finest Story in the World" begins with a chance meeting between an older, established writer and a twenty-year-old bank clerk named Charlie Mears in a London pool hall. Charlie has literary aspirations, and an apprenticeship develops between them. The younger man's early efforts are naive and unoriginal. "He rhymed 'dove' with 'love' and 'moon' with 'June' and devotedly believed that they had never been so rhymed before." But on one occasion Charlie claims to have a newfound "notion" in his head for what he calls "the most splendid story that was ever written." Charlie unfolds a tale of a primitive pirate ship, powered by galley slaves chained to the lower deck. The fate of slaves who die on the job has a flat finality: "When a man dies at his oar on that deck he isn't thrown overboard, but cut up in his chains and stuffed through the oar-hole in little pieces."

Convinced that Charlie is channeling an actual past life as a slave, the writer pays him five pounds to secure the "notion" for his own literary use. Charlie, in turn, buys the poetry books he covets, with ruinous results. Charlie arrives drunk—"Most of all he was drunk with Longfellow"— and begins to read aloud, with great enthusiasm, the opening lines of "My Lost Youth." The aspiring poet is not immune to other lyrical intoxicants—Byron, for example, or Keats. But overindulgence in these poets leads to "a confused tangle of other voices most like the mutter and hum through a City telephone in the busiest part of the day." Longfellow's effect on Charlie is quite different. "Only when the talk turned on Longfellow were the jarring cross-currents dumb." Longfellow, the narrator specifies, is "the medium in which his memory worked best."

After sharing a few of his favorite passages from Longfellow— passages that recall Kipling's own days in Boston tracking down Longfellow's house and grave—Charlie produces something else. "Well, I was thinking over the story," he tells the narrator, "and after awhile I got out of bed and wrote down on a piece of paper the sort of stuff the men might be supposed to scratch on their oars with the edges of their handcuffs." The narrator takes the sheet of resulting scratches to a specialist in Greek antiquities at the British Museum. The expert identifies Charlie's script as "extremely corrupt Greek," and offers a rough translation: "I have been—many times—overcome with weariness in this particular employment." For the narrator, Charlie's scratched message is proof that he is in the presence of something supernatural.

But is the evidence really so persuasive? Although the fact is not revealed in Kipling's story, it turns out that the line about being "many times overcome with weariness in this particular employment" is actually drawn from a sonnet of Longfellow's called "The Broken Oar." In the sonnet, a poet walks along a lonely beach in Iceland, pen in hand. The sun is setting. Seagulls circle above the crashing waves. "Then by the billows at his feet was tossed / A broken oar; and carved thereon he read, / 'Oft was I weary, when I toiled at thee.'" At this point, the reader is presented with several possible paths of interpretation. The first is that Charlie Mears is a con artist, precisely the sort of underworld cheat to be hanging out at a pool hall. He plays on the writer-narrator's willful credulity, and his ambition to make a financial killing. The second possibility is that Kipling himself is the con man, and is betting that his readers won't recognize the source of the telltale line from Longfellow. A third possibility is the hypothesis that similar circumstances produce similar results. This is the premise worked out in Kipling's later story "Wireless," in which a druggist suffering from tuberculosis, and hopelessly in love, falls into a trance and channels phrases from Keats's poem "The Eve of St. Agnes."

Whatever the correct interpretation of Charlie's effusions, the specifically biographical confession concealed in "'The Finest Story in the World'" is undoubtedly Kipling's own obsession with Longfellow. It was Kipling who was so intoxicated with Longfellow that he sought out the poet's grave in the midst of the "first big equinoctial" storm of the season.

Is it coincidence that one of the first passages Charlie quotes from Longfellow concerns "The gigantic storm-wind of the Equinox?" One of the first things Kipling did in storm-tossed Boston was to visit the wharves in order to watch the seagoing vessels return to the harbor. This would seem to be an echo of Longfellow's "My Lost Youth": "I remember the black wharves and the slips, / And the sea-tides tossing free;" When Kipling writes that Longfellow was Charlie's special "medium," stilling the "crosscurrents" of other poets, was he confessing his own debt to Longfellow? And was there a buried pun in "galley-slave," the poet chained to his task of producing poems, which would first appear in galleys, or proofs?

5.

Finally, there is the whole curious matter of Kipling's long-standing interest in psychical research and the realm of the paranormal. There is an odd interlude in "'The Finest Story in the World'" when the narrator is tempted to consult a "professional mesmerist." He wants to see if Charlie might be prompted, under hypnosis, to speak of his past lives. By chance, he encounters a Bengali law student he knows casually, someone familiar with Hindu notions of reincarnation, and seeks his advice. "It is of course an old tale with us," Grish Chunder remarks, "but to happen to an Englishman . . ."—that would indeed be rare. Chunder suggests that the narrator might "pour the ink-pool into his hand"—a reference to a method of divination known as "scrying," in which patterns are discerned in tea leaves or a crystal ball—since Charlie is clearly "a seer and he will tell us very many things."

Kipling was thoroughly familiar with Indian ideas of reincarnation and divination. He had also read widely in contemporary attempts, in both England and America, to uncover evidence of paranormal abilities, mentioning in one early story the research of Frederic Myers, founder of the British Society for Psychical Research, and his popular book

Phantasms of the Living (1886). Apart from the shenanigans of certain pro-fessional spiritualists—fakery involving secret signals, hidden trap-doors, and disguised voices—there was a serious side to this research. It was part of an ongoing attempt to make room, in a scientific and materi-alist age, for religious faith, and specifically for phenomena that could not be explained by material causes alone. Thinkers like William James were eager to reveal fraud in order to explore more aggressively what might just possibly be true, such as claims of telepathy (a word coined by Myers in 1882) or dreams that predicted the future. Mark Twain joined the Society for Psychical Research on the basis of just such a dream.

With its own rich traditions of meditation, yoga, and other spiritual practices, India was a seedbed of paranormal claims and a favored des-tination for Westerners drawn to the "wisdom of the East." European sojourners gave their own interpretive twist to Hindu ideas of reincar-nation, grafting pseudo-Darwinian notions of spiritual "evolution" to ancient beliefs regarding the progress of human souls. Simla, the sum-mer retreat that Washington resembled, became a center for such roving pilgrims and practitioners. The Kipling family, sojourning in Simla to escape the dangerous summer heat, had a close-up view of some of the exotic claimants to spiritual superiority.

Madame Blavatsky, the Russian-born founder of Theosophy and a firm believer in reincarnation, was the foremost of these. "At one time our little world was full of the aftermaths of Theosophy as taught by Madame Blavatsky to her devotees," Kipling recalled in *Something of Myself.* "My Father knew the lady and, with her, would discuss wholly secular sub-jects; she being, he told me, one of the most interesting and unscrupulous imposters he had ever met." Her trickery was evident to the researchers from the Society for Psychical Research who traveled to Simla to investi-gate, but not before the head editor of the Allahabad *Pioneer,* for which Kipling wrote, had turned the newspaper into a propaganda organ for Theosophy. Kipling's early story "In the House of Suddhoo" concerns a scam perpetrated by a spiritualist fraud.

And yet Kipling was not a firm *disbeliever* in spiritualism either. Both his mother and his mentally unstable sister, Trix, were said to have clairvoyant powers, the gift of "second sight." Kipling suspected something of the same capacity in himself. He was once asked if he believed that there was "anything to spiritualism." "There is; I know," Kipling answered. "Have nothing to do with it." Kipling's sister, as it turned out, would have a *lot* to do with it. For Charlie Mears, Longfellow was the "medium in which his memory worked best." Under the American poet's influence, the "jarring cross-currents" of the echo chamber of English poetry were, momentarily, "dumb." Medium and *Cross Currents* suggest a variety of spiritualism that Trix, ten years after the publication of her brother's famous story, fully embraced.

6.

Beginning in 1901, four women produced lengthy scripts, either by dictation or by automatic writing, while in a hypnotic trance. Two of the women, the London-based Verrells, were mother and daughter. Another, unknown to the Verrells, was Winifred Coombe Tennant, who went by the spirit-name of "Mrs. Willet." And the fourth, several thousand miles away in India, was Trix herself, who adopted the spirit-name "Mrs. Holland." When assembled, like pieces of a jigsaw puzzle, these enigmatic fragments of text from various hands could be shown to produce a coherent message, hence the term that was adopted for such bizarre phenomena: "cross correspondences."

One such case came to be known as "The Ear of Dionysius." During the summer of 1910, Mrs. Willet dictated, in a trance, a script that contained the phrase "Dionysius Ear the lobe." No explanatory context was given, but the classicist Gerald Balfour, in his book *The Ear of Dionysius*, explained that the Ear of Dionysius is "a kind of grotto hewn in the solid rock at Syracuse [on the island of Sicily] and opening on one of the stone-quarries which served as a place of captivity for Athenian prisoners of war" after the failed siege described by Thucydides. Later, the tyrant Dionysius imprisoned his enemies in the cave, which, as Balfour noted, "has the peculiar acoustic properties of a whispering gallery, and is traditionally believed to have been constructed or utilized by the Tyrant in order to overhear, himself unseen, the conversations of his prisoners." The echoing cave magnified their lamentations.

Another oracular script produced by Mrs. Willet, three years later, confirmed the location in Syracuse. "It concerned a place where slaves were kept—and Audition belongs, also Acoustics / Think of the Whispering Gally / To toil, a slave, the Tyrant—and it was called Orecchio— that's near / One ear, a one eared place." Balfour examined many more scripts, including one from Trix. There are references to "Noah and the grapes" (supposedly suggesting the captivity of Odysseus and his crew in the drunken Cyclops's cave), to the assassination of Abraham Lincoln (with John Wilkes Booth's cry of "Sic semper tyrannis" confirming Dionysius's identity as a tyrant), and so on, before an eventual solution is proposed for the baffling riddle of the messages.

The scripts, when fitted together properly, proved (according to Balfour) that two respected classical scholars who had recently died, named Verrall and Butcher, had connived from beyond the grave to send messages back to the world of the living. Their messages were intended to demonstrate beyond a reasonable doubt the survival of personal identity after death. The scripts by Trix and the other three women could be shown (with much ingenuity on the part of both the ghosts and the interpreter) to allude to an obscure monograph on Greek poetry, known only to specialists, written by a professor at Bryn Mawr, the women's college outside Philadelphia.

The case has an undeniable suggestive power. And yet what is striking to a reader of Longfellow and Kipling is how many details of *The Ear of Dionysius* seem drawn directly from "'The Finest Story in the World,'" and from Kipling's Longfellow fixation more generally. Charlie Mears, on the same evening in which the narrator discovers that Longfellow's poetry was "the medium in which his memory worked best," listens to "nearly the whole of 'The Saga of King Olaf.'" Toward the end of the evening, Charlie implores the narrator for more. "But go back, please," Charlie says, "and read 'The Skerry of Shrieks' again."

"The Skerry of Shrieks" tells how King Olaf, who introduced Christianity to Norway by force, punished a crew of pagan warlocks who intruded on his drunken Easter festivities. Olaf has them bound "foot and hand / On the Skerry's rocks." Then he sits back with his knights to listen to the "sullen roar" of the rising tide on the rocky shores of the island, mingled with other, crueler music: "Shrieks and cries of wild despair / Filled the air, / Growing fainter as they listened; / Then the bursting surge alone / Sounded on;—" It is very strange indeed to find features of Kipling's "'The Finest Story in the World'" and of Longfellow's "The Skerry of Shrieks" reproduced in the published account of *The Ear of Dionysius*. In the very first quoted passage from Mrs. Willet we find, among other things, a place where slaves are kept, a reference to the "toil" of the slaves, a reference to a "Whispering Gally" (presumably "gallery," though also punning on a galley).

As a case meant to prove spirit survival beyond the grave, *The Ear of Dionysius* would seem to offer tempting evidence. "The implications of the cross correspondences cannot be lightly dismissed," according to the historian Janet Oppenheim, "although they are still a long way from proving the reality of communications from the dead." Nonetheless, it is difficult to avoid the impression that what we are reading, in *The Ear of Dionysius*, is more a case of literary invention than of scientific exposition. Particularly conspicuous in this regard are the recurrent references to English poetry, Greek and Latin texts, and the like, all features of Kipling's tale. It would seem that the four women, listening in a trance for the echoes of eternity, heard instead the echoes of Kipling's "finest story in the world."

What the story meant for Kipling, though, had more immediate implications. He was on his way to London, at last, to make his fortune, and yet America was firmly on his mind. He had made pilgrimages to pay his respects to Twain and Longfellow, anchoring his literary ambitions firmly in American soil. He had felt himself, in the emotionally charged landscape of Emerson's Concord, "in the very beginning of things." He had tried hard to attach himself to an American family, and, specifically, to two sisters, the Taylors of Beaver, Pennsylvania. In London, not surprisingly, he would soon find another, more suitable family in which to make himself at home—an American family, of course, and again with two sisters. Literary ambition would again align itself with his emotional needs, at the dawn of a great career.

Chapter Three

A DEATH IN DRESDEN

I.

In Henry James's fictional version of the story, a brash young American, eager to escape the confines of a sleepy city in the American outback, travels to Europe in search of adventure. Daisy Miller, James's heroine, is the very embodiment of what he called the "American Girl." She delights in unnecessary risks; she forms attachments with rootless Americans and shiftless natives. Heedless of age-old conventions, Daisy is a modern young woman in every way. And yet the darker, less salubrious places of the ancient lamplit world—the legendary ruins and the picturesque shadows—attract her like a moth to moonlight. An American bachelor with the wintry name of Winterbourne, long residing in Europe, tries to shield her from danger. But daisies, as everyone knows, are particularly vulnerable in winter.

Late one night, Winterbourne, sleepless in Rome, ventures within the moldering walls of the moonlit Colosseum. To his horror, he discovers that Daisy herself has sought out the same dark refuge, in the company of an unsavory Roman suitor. There, poor Daisy catches the dread old-world fever that kills her. She is buried in the little Protestant cemetery, "by an angle of the wall of imperial Rome," James specifies, near the grave of John Keats, another doomed exile far from home. Lacerating himself for having failed to protect her, Winterbourne keeps vigil among his fellow mourners, "staring at the raw protuberance among the April daisies." And the moral is—well, what exactly? That Daisy Miller should have stayed home in Schenectady, and gone to bed early?

Only this time, in real life, the circumstances were slightly different. It was the death in Dresden of another youthful American—a slender young man not yet thirty and full of ambitious plans cut shockingly short—that set so many surprising things in motion. (One was the doomed theatrical career of Henry James; another was the marriage of Rudyard Kipling.) The young American who launched so many schemes had arrived in London in December 1888. Originally from Rochester— two hundred miles from Daisy's Schenectady—via Brattleboro, Vermont, he had spent a significant part of his life in the Far West. He knew his way among mining towns and railroads that led to nowhere. His name was Charles Wolcott (pronounced "WOOL-cut") Balestier. Huguenot sugar planters originally based in Martinique, the Balestiers had abandoned that lucrative slaveholding island with the fall of Napoléon. There was a hint of exoticism about Wolcott, an air of aristocratic origins. On his mother's side, he was related to Oliver Wolcott, an original signatory of the Declaration of Independence, and to Paul Revere, hero of Longfellow's stirring ballad about the midnight ride.

Almost his first conquest in London was Henry James. Wolcott Balestier headed the parade of young men who would play a central part in James's later life. Alice James hoped that Balestier, "the effective and the indispensable," might be a lifelong companion for her brother. But Balestier had the same fatal taste as Daisy Miller for the darker, danker corners of the Old World. Shunning the well-traveled neighborhoods of Fleet Street or the Strand, favored by publishers, he established his business offices instead in one of those pestiferous corners of ancient London. He caught a chill, like Daisy Miller—"a damnable vicious typhoid," as James wrote, "contracted in his London office, the 'picturesqueness' of which he loved." In Alice James's memorable phrase, Balestier was "swept away like a cobweb, of which gossamer substance he seems to have been himself composed."

Pale as fine porcelain and impossibly slender, Balestier resembled nothing so much as a graceful Meissen figurine, illuminated by candlelight. He died in Dresden, where Meissen is made, and he was buried, like Daisy Miller, in a small Protestant cemetery far from home. Henry James made his way—his "miserable pious pilgrimage," as he called it— to Dresden for the sad little service. Meanwhile, another of Balestier's close associates was very far away indeed. Summoned from the South Seas, Rudyard Kipling returned to mourn Balestier and to marry Balestier's sister. And that, one might say, is how it all began. But the details— the details that Henry James would have insisted upon—are what make the story interesting.

2.

Wolcott Balestier had tried his hand at many things before he came to London, and he had learned from his failures. After a year at Cornell, he invested some of his considerable Caribbean inheritance in mining interests, without success. Then he tried to spin his rambles in the West, to Colorado and down to Mexico, into literary gold. Like other writers in his cohort, he emulated, in a series of facile novels, the gentle realism of William Dean Howells, the influential editor of *The Atlantic,* who had called on American novelists to record "the more smiling aspects of life." Balestier tried to follow Howells's example in other ways. As a young man,

Howells had written a campaign biography for the underdog Republican candidate, Abraham Lincoln. His reward had been a diplomatic post in Venice. Howells, like Balestier, had Brattleboro connections. His wife, Elinor, was from Brattleboro, and her first cousin was Rutherford B. Hayes, another Brattleboro native. In addition to his Lincoln book, Howells wrote a campaign biography of Hayes, the eventual Republican victor in the contested election of 1877.

And so it was that Wolcott Balestier secured the job of writing the campaign biography for James G. Blaine, senator from Maine and the Republican candidate for president in the 1884 election. If Blaine won, as seemed likely—no Democrat had been elected to the White House since the beginning of the Civil War—Balestier might look forward to a European post. In his preface, he took care to quote Howells, fawningly, "in his admirable 'Life of Hayes,'" to the effect that "whatever is ambitious or artificial or unwise in my book is doubly my misfortune, for it is altogether false to him."

Balestier's particular challenge in the book was to defend Blaine from scandal. Known as the "Plumed Knight" to his admirers but as "Slippery Jim" to his detractors, Blaine had been a member of President Ulysses S. Grant's notoriously corrupt cabinet. He was already tainted by deals that he had previously pushed through, as Speaker of the House, in favor of railroad interests. He had apparently been rewarded for his efforts with lucrative stocks. Though never convicted, Blaine could not shake the odor of corruption attached to his name. In a chapter titled "Slander," Balestier summarily dismissed the charges. "These pages need not be burdened with a defense of Mr. Blaine against the accusations of political enemies," he wrote huffily. "They were disposed of long ago."

In the 1884 election, many lifelong Republicans crossed party lines to vote for the more honest-seeming Democratic candidate, Grover Cleveland, a pro-business lawyer from upstate New York. Such "mugwumps," as they were called—an Algonquin word popularly interpreted as meaning those with their mugs on one side of the fence and their rumps on the other—included such prominent figures as the historian Henry Adams (the grandson and great grandson of American presidents) and Mark Twain. The Blaine campaign, in turn, tried to smear Cleveland by alleging, baselessly, that he had fathered an illegitimate child, and adopted the slogan "Ma, Ma, Where's My Pa?" Cleveland won, eventually serving two terms, though not in succession, before his administration took the blame for the financial Panic of 1893.

After Blaine's defeat—a blow to his biographer's hopes as well—Balestier settled in New York, as editor of a magazine called *Tid-Bits*. He did not relinquish his hopes for a foreign posting, however. He and his publisher, John Lovell, hit on a scheme to take advantage of the absence of international copyright agreements, which had resulted in rampant piracy. This was the same problem that Mark Twain had raised so vehemently with Kipling in Elmira. The idea was for Balestier, based in London, to secure the rights to publish English books simultaneously in the United States.

In London, Balestier established his business in a peculiar, if picturesque, locale. Behind Westminster Abbey, a stone archway leads to an enclosed courtyard. Ancient buildings, among them a school for choirboys, surround a central green. Here, in serene if slightly fetid Dean's Yard, the Abbey tower looms above the rooftops. The doorway to number two—where Balestier pursued his publishing deals among the priests in their rustling robes—would have been adjacent to the stone archway. Among the austere buildings in brick and stone, it is the only one missing today, a break in the stately fabric like a gap-toothed smile. The corner building at number two apparently fell victim to persistent problems of drainage, a challenge in this damp, enclosed space.

As a literary agent, Balestier combined two talents well suited to the job: a shrewd business sense and great personal charm. He was one of the first to see the literary marketplace as an arena for speculation like any other—mining, say, or pork bellies. The writer Edmund Gosse described Balestier's data-driven command of English writers, from major

Wolcott Balestier in his London office.

figures like Thomas Hardy to "honest purveyors of deciduous fiction." Gosse wrote that he had never met anyone in the literary trade "who had anything like his power of marshaling before his memory, in due order, all the militant English writers of the moment, small as well as great." For Balestier, writers "stood in seemly rows, the names that every Englishman honors and never buys, the names that every Englishman buys and never honors. Balestier knew them all . . . knew their current value."

Gosse experienced the "thrill of attraction" on meeting Balestier, ascribing his charm to a "mixture of suave Colonial French and the strained nervous New England blood." Balestier blurred other categories as well. He was, according to Gosse, "a carefully dressed young-old man or elderly youth, clean-shaven, with smooth dark hair, thin nose, large sensitive ears, and whimsically mobile mouth." The biggest contradiction lay in the vitality of his personal presence in contrast with the frail body in which it made its precarious home. Gosse noted "the extreme pallor of the complexion" balanced "by the fire in the deeply-set dark blue eyes."

Gosse was less enthusiastic about Balestier's stock-market approach to literature, which he considered typically, and vulgarly, American. Such cold-blooded financial procedures might be familiar in what Gosse called the "whole industrial field," but in the more gentlemanly profession of publishing they were, in his judgment, "unique." Balestier brought a "sporting zest" to the literary marketplace, and what Gosse called, uneasily, his "industrial imagination." Gosse was especially startled by his young friend's "great dreams of consolidation" among the publishing houses; in this regard, and in his speculative approach to books as commodities, Balestier anticipated today's world of Amazon, publishing conglomerates, and bestseller lists. Balestier's other talent was an uncanny ability to cultivate the loyalty of the authors he sought to represent. To the insecure, he conveyed confident reassurance; to those who wished to be flattered, he could be almost insufferable in his praise. Chameleonlike, he was able to fit himself to the expectations of new acquaintances: "to each literary man and woman whom he visited he displayed a tincture of his or her own native color."

Nowhere was Balestier's lavish attention more in play than in his courtship of Henry James. "I have lately seen much of the admirably acute & intelligent young Balestier," James wrote on August 30, 1890. "I think that practically he will soon do 'everything' for me." "Everything" included reassuring James as he embarked on his riskiest venture, as a playwright. Balestier struck the perfect note: "If you will let me 'assist' at the first performance of the first play of our first dramatist ... nothing short of legal proceedings to restrain my liberty can prevent my being present."

By the summer of 1890, Balestier's activities extended beyond representing individual authors. With the German-English publisher William Heinemann, he established the firm Heinemann and Balestier, with the intention of cutting into the lucrative paperback empire of the

German Tauchnitz publishing operation in Europe. Another director in the firm was the Irish writer Bram Stoker, author of *Dracula*. Meanwhile, Balestier was hot on the trail of a "new Indian writer," whom Gosse had recommended. Gosse reported Balestier's dismissive retort when he first heard the exotic name of Rudyard Kipling. "Is it a man or a woman?" he asked. "What's its real name?" But Balestier quickly realized that Kipling was precisely the kind of author—a writer with international scope and a potentially worldwide audience—that most interested him.

Within a week, according to Gosse, Balestier had added Kipling to his "personal conquests." Within a year, he had published a volume of Kipling's Indian stories, *Mine Own People*, in the United States. He persuaded Henry James to write a preface to help sell the book. James was particularly taken with what he called Kipling's "excursions" into exotic India, which he thought brought something new and racy to the "woefully stale" precincts of English and American fiction. "A large part of his high spirits," James wrote, "comes doubtless from the amusement of such vivid, heterogeneous material, from the irresistible magic of scorching suns, subject empires, uncanny religions, uneasy garrisons and smothered-up women—from heat and color and danger and dust."

3.

Kipling had arrived in London in September 1889, fresh from his American adventures in pursuit of Mark Twain and the ghost of Longfellow. He found bohemian lodgings in Villiers Street, a short, dead-end passage that connects, in a steep descent, the Strand at Charing Cross station with the Thames River. "Primitive and passionate in its habits and population" was how Kipling described the neighborhood in *Something of Myself*; his rooms on an upper floor were "small, not over-clean or well-kept, but from my desk I could look out of my window through the fanlight of Gatti's Music-Hall entrance, across the street, almost on to its stage."

Kipling disliked London, finding it stuffy, cliquish, and cold. He had felt more energized in the United States, where the wide-open spaces and the diversity of the population reminded him of India. As he prepared, like a hero in a Balzac novel, to conquer literary London, Kipling found a kindred spirit in Wolcott Balestier, the young American on the make.

Ever mindful of the marketplace, Balestier encouraged Kipling—already an experienced hand in the writing of short stories—to try his luck with a novel. *The Light That Failed,* which Kipling dutifully wrote in haste, is the portrait of an artist named Dick Heldar, who shares many characteristics with Kipling himself. Orphaned as a child, Dick is placed in the custody of the cruel Mrs. Jennet, along with a rebellious girl named Maisie. An accident with an old pistol damages one of Dick's eyes. Both children grow up to be artists. Heldar achieves a lucrative, though journalistic, reputation depicting battle scenes while covering the British campaign in the Sudan. He returns to London to build a career as a professional artist instead, determined to eschew mere commercial success as an illustrator. There, by chance, he meets Maisie again, who lives with a mysterious "red-haired girl." In flight from London, Dick, his eyesight ruined, makes his way back to North Africa. In the midst of battle he is reunited with his loyal friend Torpenhow, and dies in his arms.

The fictional Maisie is closely modeled on a woman named Florence Garrard, whom Kipling had met through his sister, Trix. He promptly fell in love with her—he was fourteen at the time—and the obsession endured during his years as a journalist in India. The dark ending of the novel reflects both the final break with Flo and an awareness (probably only half-conscious on Kipling's part) of same-sex desire. Maisie is in love with the red-haired girl; Dick achieves true intimacy only with Torpenhow. Kipling later dismissed the novel as "only a *conte*"—a story or novella in the French style—and "not a built book," but it retains a vivid, fragmentary energy. At Balestier's urging, Kipling wrote a second version of *The Light That Failed* for the American market, with a happier ending. The book became a cult bible for younger American writers of the 1890s, such as Stephen Crane and Willa Cather, as they attempted to resist mere commercialism in their own careers.

As much for pleasure in each other's company as for any specific literary ambition, Kipling and Balestier agreed to collaborate on an adventure novel set in the two locales they knew best. It was to be a book "as American as a roller skating rink and as Indian as a juggernaut," Balestier boasted to William Dean Howells. The title of the novel, *The Naulahka*, refers to a necklace of great value—literally nine lakhs, or nine hundred thousand rupees—belonging to the ruler of the Indian state of Rajasthan. Nicholas Tarvin, the hero of the book, wants to bring the railroad to his small mining town of Topaz, in the Colorado hills. The woman of his dreams, Kate Sheriff, wants to be a medical missionary in India. Tarvin hits on a risky plan to get the railroad and the girl: he will travel to Rajasthan and steal the necklace, which he will then present to the acquisitive wife of the railroad chairman, who has agreed, in exchange, to influence her husband to extend the railroad to Topaz. "Kipling and I have been wading deep into our story lately," Balestier informed Howells on February 18, 1891, "and have written rather more than two thirds of it. It begins in the West where I have a free hand for several chapters. Then we lock arms and march upon India." Henry James had been "reading the first part of it," Balestier added, "and professes himself delighted with the Western atmosphere."

During all this feverish collaboration, there was often a third presence in the room, Balestier's twenty-seven-year-old sister, Caroline who kept house in their Kensington rooms. Carrie had traveled in the West with her brother and was capable of many things of which English girls were ignorant. She promptly taught Kipling to type. "It's so nice to have him in the typewriter fold," she told her sister, Josephine, back in Vermont, adding that Kipling was "so refreshingly unEnglish." The three were inseparable. "He keeps his clothes partly here and insists that a place be placed for him always so it is at dinner and supper," Carrie reported. Soon,

Caroline Balestier at the time of her wedding.

Josephine, the younger sister, arrived as well, and was similarly smitten with Kipling, in a replay of his sisters fixation.

4.

"He amazes me by his precocity and various endowments," Henry James wrote of Kipling that winter. "But he alarms me by his copiousness and haste." Meanwhile, Kipling was sending out signals to his family that he was suffering from overwork and a recurrence of the kind of psycho-logical symptoms that had plagued him since childhood, when he was prey to hallucinations during his turbulent years away from his parents. That spring, news reached the Macdonald sisters that their brother Harry, the black sheep of the family, was dying of throat cancer in New

York. A sea journey for Rudyard, in the company of his uncle Fred Macdonald, a Methodist minister, would combine family duty with a therapeutic respite. Two days before the ship carrying his brother and nephew
docked in New York, Harry died at the age of fifty-five. Fred stayed on
to deal with his brother's affairs while Kipling discovered that Balestier's
hard work in promoting his career was paying off in America. Pursued
by New York reporters as a rising celebrity, he hurried back to London.

A more satisfying refuge was Wolcott Balestier's seaside cottage on
the Isle of Wight, where Kipling came for a summer visit in July. It is
easy to imagine the two young men, collaborating on their ramshackle
novel, staring out to sea from the diamond-shaped island—"the little
penciled island," as Henry James called it—where two prominent light-
houses protected ships in the English Channel from running aground.
Both men needed rest. Balestier complained that he wasn't feeling well
and left the daily operations of his London business in the care of Will
Cabot, a Brattleboro family friend. Heinemann, Balestier's partner,
wasn't pleased with the arrangement. "Your idea of running a London
office from the Isle of Wight is about as sensible as steering a ship in a
storm from the top of a lighthouse," he wrote.

The suggestive image of the lighthouse was on Kipling's mind as well.
Though doctors had told him, during the summer of 1891, to avoid any
work of his own, he wrote a strange and powerful story, "The Disturber
of Traffic," about a lighthouse keeper who slowly goes mad. The narrator
dons "a pair of black glass spectacles" at the start of the tale and contem-
plates the blinding warning light. "One star came out over the cliffs," he
notes, "the waters turned lead-color, and St. Cecilia's light shot out across
the sea in eight long pencils that wheeled slowly from right to left, melted
into one beam of solid light laid down directly in front of the tower, dis-
solved again into eight, and passed away." The long pencils and lead-
colored water suggest handwriting, as though an exhausted writer,
suffering from eyestrain, is puzzling over his manuscript.

By the late summer, Kipling's symptoms of overwork—mania, panic, and occasional hallucinations—were sufficiently alarming that his doctor recommended an extended sea voyage to recuperate, something more relaxing than the aborted trip to New York. Meanwhile, his relations with Carrie Balestier seem to have taken a more serious turn, and he needed time and distance to decide what precisely he should do about them. Kipling now envisioned a second voyage around the world, in the opposite direction from his 1889 journey, with a leisurely ramble through the South Seas, where he hoped, at long last, to meet Robert Louis Stevenson, who was rumored to be dying in Samoa.

As he prepared for departure, Kipling wrote a yearning love poem, dedicated to Wolcott Balestier, titled "The Long Trail."

> There's a whisper down the field where the year has
>   shot her yield,
> And the ricks stand grey to the sun,
> Singing: "Over then, come over, for the bee has quit
>   the clover,
> And your English summer's done."

If winter was coming to England, Kipling wrote, there were warmer climes elsewhere. "You have heard the beat of the off-shore wind, / And the thresh of the deep-sea rain; / You have heard the song—how long? How long? / Pull out on the trail again!" So it was that on August 22, Rudyard Kipling, having already achieved precocious fame at the age of twenty-five, sailed out of England to begin yet another journey around the world.

Henry James relished the possibility of a meeting between Kipling and Stevenson. "That little black demon of a Kipling," he wrote Stevenson, "will have perhaps leaped upon your silver strand by the time this reaches you—he publicly left England to embrace you, many weeks ago—carrying literary genius out of the country with him in his pocket." Henry Adams, the historian who had recently arrived in London from his own Pacific travels, sounded a similar theme. "Except Stevenson and Rudyard Kipling, who are both in the South Seas from whence I have only just emerged, I hear of neither poet, novelist, historian, essayist or philosopher of note."

Visiting Balestier on the Isle of Wight in late August, Henry James was alarmed by his friend's precarious health. But the publishing empire that Balestier had dreamed up with Heinemann, which they called the English Library, required his attention. He planned to meet Albert Brockhaus, their German associate, in Leipzig. Already suffering from a fever when he arrived in Berlin, Balestier made an unplanned detour to Dresden, to be cared for by friends of the Cabot family of Brattleboro. Meanwhile, his mother and his two sisters, sojourning in Paris, were urgently summoned to his bedside.

Informed by Carrie of the dire situation, Henry James came immediately, arriving just in time for the funeral—Balestier had died on December 6, 1891—arranged in the "bristling alien cemetery" by the amiable American consul, Mr. Knoop. "The English chaplain read the service with sufficient yet not offensive sonority, and the arrangements were of an admirable, decorously grave German kind," James reported. "The little cemetery," he added, in a touch reminiscent of *Daisy Miller,* "is suburbanly dreary, but I have seen worse."

Among the small knot of mourners, James found Balestier's mother and his sister Josephine "altogether wonderful and so absolutely composed," but it was "poor little concentrated, passionate Carrie" who particularly impressed him. The two of them traveled back from the cemetery in a black and silver coach of their own, since, as James pointedly put it, "she wanted to talk to me." James found Carrie "remarkable in her force, acuteness, capacity and courage—and in the intense—almost manly—nature of her emotion." She was, he concluded, "a worthy sister of poor dear big-spirited, only-by-death-quenchable Wolcott." What Carrie Balestier wanted to talk about with Henry James was her plan to marry Rudyard Kipling.

5.

Henry James lingered in the "grey rococo capital," frequenting Dresden's great art museum. "Everything human is shabby here except Raphael's Divine Madonna *and* the bull-necked military," he wrote. For James, everything was darkened by Balestier's death. Like Winterbourne in *Daisy Miller*, keeping vigil in the Protestant cemetery, James had failed to save the young American in his charge, and had ended up, instead, at "his ugly and alien German grave." He tried to persuade himself that Balestier had gone to Germany on a therapeutic holiday rather than to pump up sales for James's books. Balestier had taken care of Henry James. Helplessly and much too late, poor Henry James now tried to take care of Balestier, only to find that his sister Carrie—equipped with the will, the skill, and the larger sense of what had to be done—had everything firmly in hand, including her plan to marry, as soon as humanly possible, her brother's best friend.

Henry Adams set the wintry scene in London on January 13, 1892. "I sat with Henry James an hour or two yesterday afternoon and found him in double trouble between the death of his friend Balestier and the steady decline of his sister," Adams wrote. "Everyone has influenza, or has had it, or expects to have it." Kipling had arrived in London three days earlier. He had planned to spend the holidays and his twenty-sixth birthday in Lahore with his parents. But on Christmas Eve, he received the terrible news of Balestier's death, in a telegram from Carrie, and immediately set sail for London. Meanwhile, rumors had reached Beatty Balestier, in Brattleboro, to the effect that Kipling was going to marry one of his sisters. It wasn't at all clear to Beatty, or to Kipling's friends in London, *which* sister.

Everything about the wedding, following so closely on the heels of the funeral, struck the participants as strange. Its shocking haste, in particular, took everyone by surprise. Kipling had been in London for barely a week when the wedding was held, at All Souls Church on Langham Place, on January 18. If there had been an understanding between Kipling and Carrie, reached before his departure for the South Seas, the couple had kept it a secret even from their closest friends. Was there a long-simmering romance, hidden to all? Or had Wolcott Balestier, dying in Dresden, exacted a deathbed promise from his sister to marry his best friend?

The wedding was more like an extension of Balestier's burial than a reprieve from it. Carrie's mother and sister were laid up with influenza; so were Kipling's aunts, Georgiana and Agnes, the wives of the distinguished painters Edward Burne-Jones and Edward Poynter, respectively. It is probably just as well that Kipling's parents, back in India, did not attend, since upon meeting Carrie on an earlier visit to London they had been unimpressed. Kipling's father, echoing James's assessment of her "manly" emotions, had said that strong-willed Carrie "would have made a good man." Gosse attended and so did Heinemann, arriving late with a bouquet of flowers.

It was left to Henry James to give the bride away—"a queer office for me to perform," as he remarked. The whole occasion, as James summed it up, was yet another indication of what he called "the ubiquity of the American girl." In preparation for his honeymoon, Kipling hurriedly changed the pronouns in the love poem that he had written for Balestier. He dedicated "The Long Trail" to Carrie instead, addressing her as "Dear Lass" rather than "Dear Lad."

On February 2, the Kiplings left London on the first leg of their projected around-the-world honeymoon. Four imposing men had loyally congregated to wish them farewell: Henry James, Edmund Gosse, William Heinemann, and Bram Stoker. With Carrie's sister, Josephine, and their mother, they then boarded the *SS Teutonic* in Liverpool.

"I saw the Rudyard Kiplings off by the *Teutonic* the other day," James wrote to his brother William. "She was poor Wolcott Balestier's sister and is a hard devoted capable little person whom I don't in the least understand his marrying. It's a union of which I don't forecast the future though I gave her away at the altar in a dreary little wedding with an attendance simply of four men." He added a handsome, though qualified, compliment: "Kipling strikes me personally as the most complete man of genius (as distinct from fine intelligence) that I have ever known."

As something of a wedding gift, James had secured a suitable traveling companion for the Kiplings. Henry Adams, returning to his home in Washington, was also on the *Teutonic*. During the long days on board, Kipling made final corrections to *The Naulahka*—the novel he had written with Balestier that would now serve as his dear friend's memorial—and wrote verses for its chapter headings. Each evening, the two writers met for dinner. Like Mark Twain before him, Adams was astonished by his new friend's verbal dexterity. Kipling "dashed over the passenger his exuberant fountain of gaiety and wit—as though playing a garden hose on a thirsty and faded begonia." After the shocking suicide of his wife, Clover, a gifted photographer who had killed herself by ingesting the cyanide she used to develop her prints, Adams had traveled to Japan to restore some emotional and spiritual balance to his life. Mourning his dead wife, he told a reporter in Nebraska that he was pursuing nirvana. "It's out of season," the reporter responded. The honeymooning Kiplings, who planned to travel on to Japan after a brief stopover in New England, were hoping for a better harvest.

land from Carrie's brother, Beatty, as they contemplated a possible vacation house in Vermont. From the elevated site, they could see Mount Monadnock—which "came to mean everything that was helpful, healing, and full of quiet," Kipling wrote—and celebrated the occasion by building a snowman. "For the honor of Monadnock there was made that afternoon an image of snow of Gautama Buddha," Kipling wrote with mock solemnity, "something too squat and not altogether equal on both sides, but with an imperial and reposeful waist." At that moment, some men came up the road in a wood-sledge and confronted the Buddha. Of this strange meeting of East and West, Kipling remarked, "the amazed comments of two Vermont farmers on the nature and properties of a swag-bellied god are worth hearing."

Then, the epic wedding journey resumed in earnest, like an open parenthesis with no predetermined closure in sight: across the Canadian wilderness to Vancouver and then the long Pacific crossing. Kipling hoped to travel all the way around the world, with a stop at Samoa to pay their respects to Robert Louis Stevenson, a long-cherished dream. His last attempt had been interrupted by news of Wolcott's death. They might even visit Bombay, and Kipling's parents, before the eventual return home.

For Carrie Kipling, Japan had a special significance. Her maternal grandfather, Erasmus Peshine Smith, was an expert in banking and international law. He was the first foreign adviser hired by the emperor, or mikado, to help Japan, long isolated from the West, catch up with the modern world. Commodore Matthew Perry's heavily armed Black Ships had entered Edo Bay in 1853, and demanded that Japan open its ports to American ships and American trade. The famous "opening" was a humiliation for Japan; Smith and other foreigners were enlisted to right the balance. Smith remained in Tokyo for five years, overseeing treaties and establishing the nation's banking system. He also represented Japan in a landmark case in which a Peruvian ship, loaded with a cargo of 230 so-called "coolies" from China and other parts of Asia, was wrecked off the Japanese coast. The ship's occupants were freed after Smith argued that such human trafficking violated international agreements against the slave trade. In accord with his official status, Peshine Smith proudly dressed as a samurai on ceremonial occasions, with the two swords appropriate to his rank. Kipling had seen the impressive swords in his brother-in-law Beatty's house in Vermont.

2.

A few doors down from the Grand Hotel stood the Overseas Club, where Kipling liked to read the international newspapers on hot afternoons. With its ample veranda equipped with a telescope for viewing incoming ships, the club was a fine example of the colonial outpost so often portrayed by Joseph Conrad—in Hong Kong, Rangoon, or Kipling's native Bombay. In such places, the vagabonds whom Kipling referred to as "Outside Men" (a literal translation, presumably, of the Japanese term for foreigner, *gaijin*) could find momentary respite and camaraderie. "A strong family likeness runs through both buildings and members," Kipling wrote, "and a large and careless hospitality is the note." According to Kipling, there was "always the same open-doored, high-ceiled house, with matting on the floors; the same come and go of dark-skinned servants, and the same assembly of men talking horse or business, in raiment that would fatally scandalize a London committee, among files of newspapers from a fortnight to five weeks old."

Kipling was summoning a world nostalgically recalled—open doors, high ceilings, and servants—from his infancy in Bombay, as evoked in "Song of the Wise Children":

> We shall go back by the boltless doors,
> To the life unaltered our childhood knew—
> To the naked feet on the cool, dark floors,
> And the high-ceiled rooms that the Trade blows through.

He also knew from his childhood that disaster could intrude at any moment. During his lonely years in England, at the foster home he called "The House of Desolation," he found momentary solace in the fantasy world of books, enacting scenes from *Robinson Crusoe* in a mildewy basement. "My apparatus was a coconut shell strung on a red cord, a tin trunk, and a piece of packing-case which kept off any other world," he recalled. "Thus fenced about, everything inside the fence was quite real. The magic," he added, "lies in the ring or fence that you take refuge in."

For Kipling, the veneer of refuge at the Overseas Club masked the precarious lives of the Outside Men, even as childhood was surrounded by unsuspected dangers. He began an upbeat passage with a rhyme: "Consuls and judges of the Consular Courts meet men over on leave from the China ports, or it may be Manila, and they all talk tea, silk, banking, and exchange with its fixed residents." But the description moves abruptly from comfort to disaster: "Everything is always as bad as it can possibly be, and everybody is on the verge of ruin. That is why, when they have decided that life is no longer worth living, they go down to the skittle-alley—to commit suicide."

3.

On his previous visit to Japan, when he was circling the world in 1889 on his way to the United States, Kipling had been an Outside Man himself. And it was in Japan during that earlier journey that he had experienced something deeply unsettling, an early intimation that at any time, and with no advance warning, one could suddenly find oneself *on the verge of ruin*. He was twenty-three at the time—unknown, unmarried, and equipped with a passport identifying him, like some Tibetan beggar, as Radjerd Kyshrig. "Write your name distinctly," he admonished himself, not for the last time. He had taken a room at the Yaami Hotel, a weather-beaten enclave supposedly in the Western style, favored by foreign tourists. Notched among the forested eastern hills of Kyoto, the old capital city of Japan, the ramshackle hotel was surrounded by ancient Buddhist temples. It was spring, the famous cherry trees were in full bloom, and a whole sea of blossoms—the *sakura* of the plaintive song the local Japanese schoolchildren sang—unfurled below his window.

Kipling had come up the coast from the port city of Nagasaki, making his way overland to Kyoto. Like many other travelers, Kipling viewed Japan as a realm of perfect taste, perfect beauty, as though woodblock prints had miraculously assumed three dimensions. He glimpsed, from the porthole of his ship as it approached Nagasaki, two islands amid the waves. "This morning, after the sorrows of the rolling night, my cabin porthole showed me two great grey rocks, studded and streaked with green, and crowned by two stunted blue-black pines." Kipling had seen enough Japanese art to know what he was looking at: art transformed into life. "Below the rocks a boat, that might have been carved sandalwood for color and delicacy, was shaking out an ivory-white frilled sail to the wind of the morning. An indigo-blue boy with an old ivory face and a musical voice was hauling on a rope." Rock, tree, and boat," Kipling concluded of this scene straight out of Hokusai, "made a panel from a Japanese screen."

And yet it was not a Japanese artist that the stunted pines and the rippling waves recalled for Kipling. Instead, it was a few lines from his beloved Emerson:

> Thou canst not wave thy staff in air,
> Or dip thy paddle in the lake,
> But it carves the bow of beauty there,
> And ripples in rhymes the oar forsake.

The meaning of these mysterious lines seems to be that when we are in the right mood, there is an intimate correspondence between our human selves and the surrounding landscape. At such magical moments, poetry is somehow built into what we see, the rhyming ripples and the sculpted features of pine and mountain, as in the forested hills of Kyoto, where Kipling slept soundly in his quiet hotel.

4.

And then, suddenly, in the first light of morning, the whole hillside seemed to be rolling, *undulating*, as though to shake the delicate pink and white flowers loose from their jagged black branches. "Very early in the dawn, before the nesting sparrows were awake, there was a sound in the air which frightened me out of my virtuous sleep," he wrote. "It was a lisping mutter—very deep and entirely strange." Kipling conferred on the event, after the fact, an oddly domestic, even maternal, aspect—the nesting sparrows, the sleeping man-child, the lisping mutter (or mother) gently shaking her child awake: "And the lisp of the split banana-frond," as he wrote in the nostalgic poem about his Bombay childhood, "that talked us to sleep when we were small."

All is well, until it's not.

At breakfast, when the ominous shaking had finally subsided, hotel staff members showed Kipling, with proper ceremony, the path that led to the source of the earthquake. Kipling "stepped through the violet-studded long grass into forgotten little Japanese cemeteries—all broken pillars and lichened tablets." There he found, "under a cut in the hillside, the big bell of Kyoto—twenty feet of green bronze hung inside a fantastically roofed shed of wooden beams." It was as though Kipling had entered, for a moment, the echoing space of a haiku, in which temple bells have resounded through the centuries, from haiku masters Basho to Shiki. One can even imagine the wording: "Cherry blossom dawn. / I awake to an earthquake: / Chion temple bell."

Kipling found himself, that morning, in the sublime presence of the legendary temple bell of Chion-in, all seventy-four tons of it, the largest cast-iron bell in all of Japan. "A knuckle rapped lightly on the lip," he noted, "made the great monster breathe heavily, and the blow of a stick started a hundred shrill-voiced echoes round the darkness of its dome." As he looked on, half a dozen men heaved the great battering ram of the knocker against the cavernous belly of the bell. "I endured twenty strokes and removed myself," Kipling wrote, "not in the least ashamed of mistaking the sound for an earthquake."

5.

Rising sharply above the busy streets of Yokohama, and buffered from the crowds by a canal lined with boats, stood the fashionable Bluff, where Europeans and Americans had their homes, their exclusive private clubs, and their cemetery. It was here, after a few nights at the Grand Hotel, that the Kiplings settled in, welcomed into the home of a friendly English merchant, E. J. Hunt, and his wife, whom they had met on their passage from Vancouver. "They made us more than welcome in their house," Kipling wrote, "and saw to it that we should see Japan in wisteria and peony time." Seeing Japan entailed visits to the curio shops and photographers' studios of Yokohama. It also meant the obligatory side trip to Nikko, the mountain resort to the north where the Tokugawa shoguns, the fierce warlords who had ruled Japan during its centuries of isolation, were buried. They spent a night in Tokyo en route to Nikko, but not long enough, as Kipling explained to the young British attaché, Cecil Spring Rice, for social calls. To the south, they visited the baths at picturesque Miyanoshita, a craggy resort of pine-forested cliffs in view of Mount Fuji.

But seeing Japan mainly meant, for the young couple, lounging in the Hunts' garden on a corner of the Bluff overhanging the harbor, and admiring—as though the view had been composed by Hiroshige—how the curving eaves on the house "consorted with the sweep of the pine branches." The Kiplings enjoyed "a garden that is not ours, but belongs to a gentleman in slate-colored silk, who, solely for the sake of the picture, condescends to work as a gardener, in which employ he is sweeping delicately a welt of fallen cherry blossoms from under an azalea aching to burst into bloom." Kipling also noted the "steep stone steps, of the color that nature ripens through long winters," that led up to the garden. With its overriding theme of ripeness after a long winter, and the azalea aching to burst into blossom, the whole passage is written in code. For Carrie was pregnant, and there was every reason to lounge in the garden rather than join the American tourists down in the shopping districts below the Bluff.

6.

The narrow streets of Yokohama smelled of tea. "All along the sea face," Kipling wrote of his daily walk down the Bluff, "is an inspiring smell of the finest new-mown hay, and canals are full of boats loaded up with the boxes jostling down to the harbor." The newly harvested tea, from choice locales like Uji and Shizuoka, was unloaded and carried through the streets to the great factory, where it was laboriously dried (or "fired") by hand, before being packaged for the insatiable American market. For Kipling, the whole process in the tea factory had a symbolic aura. It became in his mind a magical scene of metamorphosis, of life, and, more alarmingly, of death:

> The factory floors are made slippery with the tread of bare-footed coolies, who shout as the tea whirls through its transformations. The over-note to the clamor—an uncanny thing too—is the soft rustle-down of the tea itself—stacked in heaps, carried in baskets, dumped through chutes, rising and falling in the long

troughs where it is polished, and disappearing at last into the heart of the firing-machine—always this insistent whisper of moving dead leaves. Steam-sieves sift it into grades, with jarrings and thumpings that make the floor quiver, and the thunder of steam-gear is always at its heels; but it continues to mutter unabashed till it is riddled down into the big, foil-lined boxes and lies at peace.

There is that reassuring word "mutter" again, and the image of lying at peace. After the violent, uncanny transformation of the tea, all seems to be well. Until it isn't.

On June 3, Kipling was fast asleep in the early dawn. Suddenly, he was wide awake. He saw, with horror, that his empty boots on the floor were *moving*. They made the strangest sound—"sat and played toccatas stately at the clavichord," as in one of Robert Browning's poems. But no, that was only the washstand rattling. Then it—whatever *it* was— intensified: "a clock fell and a wall cracked, and heavy hands caught the house by the roof-pole and shook it furiously." It sounded as though batteries of artillery were charging up the Bluff. This time, he was certain. It really *was* an earthquake.

Terrified, the Kiplings rushed out of the house and into the garden, "where a tall cryptomeria waggled its insane head back and forth with an 'I told you so' expression: though not a breath was stirring." The servants in the garden laughed at the terrified visitors, an unwelcome reminder, for Kipling, of the embarrassing episode with the temple bell. "Then came the news, swift borne from the business quarters below the hill, that the coolies of certain factories had fled shrieking at the first shock, and that all the tea in the pans was burned to a crisp." That, Kipling reflected, was consolation for "undignified panic." Again, Kipling summoned all of his verbal resources to give an adequate frame to his response. "To preserve an equal mind when things are hard is good," he wrote, "but he who has fumbled desperately at bolted jalousies [Venetian blinds] that will not open while a whole room is being tossed in a blanket does not know how hard it is to find any sort of mind at all."

The first part of the sentence—"To preserve an equal mind when things are hard is good"—was a loose translation from the Roman poet Horace, one of Kipling's favorite writers. Horace strikes a stoic note: "Aequam memento rebus in arduis / servare mentem." The challenge of preserving an equal mind in perilous circumstances would become one of Kipling's greatest themes. "If—," his most popular poem, praises those who can "keep their heads" when others, less levelheaded, are "losing theirs and blaming it on you."

7.

Kipling's third Japanese earthquake, a figurative one this time, struck just six days later, on June 9. It was a date he would never forget. It was raining, raining hard, and the narrow streets were brimming, as Kipling put it, with "gruelly mud." He made his way down the Bluff, as usual, and across the canal to the Bund and the Overseas Club, to read the newspapers with the Outside Men. Then, he proceeded to the Yokohama branch of his bank to withdraw money for one of his sightseeing excursions. "Why not take more?" asked the manager, with a gently insinuating tone. "It will be just as easy."

Worried about the wisdom of carrying too much cash on his person, Kipling missed the manager's hint. When he returned to the Bund later in the day, there was an alarming notice on the door informing customers that the bank had suspended payment. "The noise of barring up continued, the rain fell, and the notice stared down the wet street." Afraid of a thief, Kipling was waylaid instead by a colossal bank failure.

Like a tsunami, news of the financial disaster "came out of the sea unheralded," Kipling wrote, "an evil born with all its teeth." He was deeply impressed with the equanimity—the equal mind—with which the Outside Men at the club greeted the loss of their life savings. "A man passed stiffly and some one of the group turned to ask lightly, 'Hit, old man?' 'Like hell,' he said, and went on biting his unlit cigar." For the Kiplings, there was the additional irony that Carrie's own grandfather had established the foundations of Japanese banking. And now, those foundations were shaken to the core. The tremor of 1892, and the global instability that culminated in the Panic of 1893, reverberated around the world. "It is wholesome and tonic to realize the powerlessness of man in the face of these little accidents," Kipling concluded. "The heir of all the ages, the annihilator of time and space, who politely doubts the existence of his Maker, hears the roof-beams crack and strain above him and scuttles about like a rabbit in a stoppered warren."

Kipling's entire fortune was in the bank. Flat broke, he was about to be a father. It was time for the honeymooners, however reluctantly, to cut their journey short. "Retreat—flight if you like—was indicated," as Kipling wrote dryly. Thomas Cook's travel agency generously granted them two return vouchers to Vancouver, en route to Vermont.

8.

Before their departure, Rudyard and Carrie made a pilgrimage to the great bronze statue of the Buddha at Kamakura—the model for their snow Buddha in Brattleboro—twenty miles distant from Yokohama through the carefully ordered grid of rice fields. The colossal Buddha, seated in a lotus position, was himself a monument of survival amid accidents and disasters. Cast in the thirteenth century, the statue weighed ninety-three tons. (The Great Bell of Kyoto, that other marvel of cast bronze, weighed seventy-four tons.) It was originally protected by a wooden hall, which was destroyed by a storm in 1334, rebuilt, and again damaged by another storm in 1369. Finally, a tsunami—induced by yet another earthquake—washed away the entire building in 1498, never to be rebuilt after the flood. Henceforth, the statue was left unprotected from the elements, "facing the sea," as Kipling wrote, "to hear the centuries go by."

For Kipling, the Great Buddha, sitting in silence through storm and flood, embodied the "equal mind" that Horace had praised. Now, the statue, "a visible god sitting in the garden of a world made new," endured, with equal stoicism, a flood of tourists from all nations, buying photographs of themselves "standing on his thumbnail." To his prose evocation of the long-suffering Buddha, Kipling appended a poem.

The Buddha at Kamakura, photograph by Felix Beato (c. 1867–69).

Kipling's poem, "Buddha at Kamakura," was a plea for intolerant Christians—who invoked the "Narrow Way," and envisioned sinners sacrificed at Tophet and on the Day of Judgment—to show respect to the Buddha:

> O ye who tread the Narrow Way
> By Tophet-flare to Judgment Day,
> Be gentle when "the heathen" pray
> To Buddha at Kamakura!

As an additional sign of respect, Kipling placed the accent correctly on "Kamakura," with a light emphasis on the second syllable rather than, in the English manner, on the first and third.

> The grey-robed, gay-sashed butterflies
> That flit beneath the Master's eyes.
> He is beyond the Mysteries
> But loves them at Kamakura.

Rejecting the Crucifixion and the harsh tenets of Calvinism, under which he himself had suffered as a foster child in England, Kipling ended the poem with a probing question:

> But when the morning prayer is prayed,
> Think, ere ye pass to strife and trade,
> Is God in human image made
> No nearer than Kamakura?

These verses in praise of the Buddha at Kamakura, hastily written to fill out a newspaper column, would remain, for Kipling, the lasting gift of his second journey to Japan. They expressed, more fully than anything he had found in Christian liturgy or practice, his maturing view of how to respond to the vicissitudes of life, whether triumph or disaster. A decade later, he would use stanzas from the poem as epigraphs to the opening chapters of his great novel *Kim*. The book is structured as a pilgrimage, in which a Tibetan lama goes in search of the river where the Buddha's arrow landed.

Kipling's own experience in Japan could hardly be compared with what the bronze Buddha at Kamakura had endured, from storm and tsunami. He himself had survived three earthquakes—one imaginary, one real, and one metaphorical. But the Buddha gave him an inspiring emblem. And now, like the Buddha at Kamakura, Kipling resolutely faced the Pacific, and contemplated fatherhood and the future with an equal mind.

Chapter Five

An Ark for Josephine

I.

The recent earthquakes in Japan—the shaking hillside in Yokohama followed by the devastating bank failure—weighed on Kipling's mind during the long train ride from Vancouver back to Vermont in July of 1892. "We had received the first shock of our young lives," he wrote. The shock was partly financial; it had wiped out his savings. But the tremor had struck more deeply, at an emotional and even existential level. In February, he had bought, on impulse, ten acres of land near the Brattleboro-Dummerston line from his brother-in-law, Beatty Balestier, with a view to a vacation home at some future time. With the interrupted honeymoon, what had once seemed a harmless lark was now in deadly earnest. Kipling needed a secure place to work; he needed a safe place for his wife and child; he needed a way to make money, and *fast.*

The Balestiers in Brattleboro had been alerted to the crisis in Japan.

A telegram was waiting in Montreal from Anna Balestier, Carrie's mother, with the encouraging news that an empty cottage was available at Bliss Farm, down the road from Maplewood, the big farmhouse where Beatty, his wife, Mai, and their baby daughter lived. Abandoned houses abounded in the economically depressed neighborhood, Kipling soon learned, "some decaying where they stood; others already reduced to a stone chimneystack or mere green dimples still held by an undefeated lilac-bush." Bliss Cottage had served as temporary lodging for a hired man and then as a writing studio for a playwright named Steele Mac-Kaye. Kipling's new workroom, he reported, "was seven feet by eight, and from December to April the snow lay level with its window-sill." For three weeks, the Kiplings worked nonstop to winterize the house. They bought, secondhand, a furnace for the damp cellar, cutting holes in the thin floors for its eight-inch pipes. "Why we were not burned in our beds each week of the winter I never can understand," Kipling remarked.

Kipling's memories of Bliss Cottage during that first winter have a ritualistic feel, as though, with a wizard's wand, he was warding off evil spirits to keep his family safe. He lined the drafty windowsills with spruce boughs. When the lead pipe froze, he and Carrie slipped down to the basement in their coonskin coats and warmed it with a candle.

As they outfitted the cottage with furniture bought on a quick trip to New York, they found themselves living in a miniature abode seemingly built for fairies rather than people. The attic bedroom was too small for a cradle, so they laid out a trunk-tray instead. Two days before New Year's Eve, in three feet of snow, Josephine Kipling was born.

2.

Soon after his arrival in Brattleboro, Kipling wrote to Mary Mapes Dodge, editor of the popular American children's magazine *St. Nicholas*, to propose a batch of new stories, destined for an eventual book, under the title *Noah's Ark Tales.* The biblical story of Noah—that epic of devastation on a grand scale followed, under the sign of the rainbow, by new and hopeful beginnings—had crystallized in Kipling's mind as singularly appropriate to his own precarious situation in his newly adopted country. And besides, a collection of animal tales, under the comforting aegis of Noah's Ark, seemed just the right gift for a newborn child.

The first of the Noah's Ark Tales that Kipling was writing for little Josephine were "Mowgli's Brothers" and "Toomai of the Elephants." Both stories would become chapters in *The Jungle Book,* completed during the following year. Kipling submitted three other tales to *St. Nicholas,* about a camel, a whale, and a rhinoceros, the first installments of what would eventually become his *Just So Stories.* The stories were so named not because they were about how certain odd animals had ended up "just so," but because Josephine insisted that each story be told exactly the same way—hence, "just so." Kipling's narrative style, packed with playful rhymes and puns, preserved the illusion of a parent reading or improvising, aloud. "In the sea, once upon a time, O my Best Beloved, there was a Whale, and he ate fishes," he would begin. "He ate the starfish and the garfish, and the crab and the dab, and the plaice and the dace, and the skate and his mate, and the mackereel and the pickereel, and the really truly twirly-whirly eel."

Kipling's Noah's Ark Tales had thus split in two, with one stream of animal stories entering *The Jungle Book* while another stream turned into his *Just So Stories.* Yet a third narrative current came out of the original concept of the Noah's Ark Tales. Kipling playfully asked Dodge if she had ever heard the story of "the small boy who made himself a Noah's ark on an Indian tank and filled it with animals, and how they wouldn't agree, and how the dove wouldn't fly for the olive branch, and how Noah was ingloriously lugged to the bank with all his ark and spanked." Or had she heard "of the small boy who got a blessing and a ghost-dagger from a Tibetan lama who came down from Tibet in search of a miraculous river that washed away all sin (the river that gushed out when the

Bodhisat's arrow struck the ground) and how these two went hunting for it together—the old priest with his priestly tam o'shanter hat and the young English child?"

Despite the parallel wording about the small boy, Kipling seems to be referring here to two different stories. The first is about a boy who gets into trouble when he plays with a toy Noah's Ark in a tank, or pond. The other story is the first reference to what would become Kipling's great novel *Kim*, about an English (later Irish) child who spies for the British colonial authorities while he accompanies a Tibetan Buddhist priest on his pilgrimage across India. The dawning concept of *Kim* was apparently associated, for Kipling, with the story of Noah's Ark. One can easily imagine the clever and resourceful Kim himself trying, as a young boy, to make the toy Ark float and the toy dove fly. The novel that emerged a decade later was, as Edward Said noted, so full of the diverse population of India that it might itself be considered a "veritable Noah's Ark."

3.

Josephine Kipling was given an actual toy Noah's Ark, accompanied by 126 animal and human figures, when she was eighteen months old. It soon became her favorite plaything. Made by hand in Germany, such toy Arks were a fixture of Victorian childhood, a reminder, perhaps, that there was an alternative explanation for animal survival to Darwin's. The roof could be opened to reveal the colorfully painted animals inside. The dove, with an olive branch in her mouth, often perched on top of the Ark. Kipling was fascinated by how such toys were made. "Do you know how the beasts are profiled and cut out of a revolving hollow disc of wood?" he asked his Canadian friend Robert Barr, a journalist and editor. "One animal to each section without waste."

Josephine's Ark was a gift from Kipling's aunt Louisa Baldwin, presented on a visit the Kiplings made to England to visit his parents, during the summer of 1894. Kipling sent his aunt profuse thanks: "The first thing I did after unpacking was to arrange them two by two in the proper way and then with paternal foresight I sucked a red and white moo-cow hard," he wrote. "After much sucking she turned slightly paler and so to make all certain the Pater varnished the whole hundred and twenty six of 'em and the Doctor looked in and he must needs play with them while they were lying all sticky on the window seat and then I arranged them scientifically once more and said how amusing a thing a Noah's Ark must be for such as cared for childish things." The assembled adults decided that baby Jo was too small for "so much natural history all of a heap," but Jo had other ideas. According to Kipling, she "gathered them to her heart as many as she could hold and put the cows to bed in a spare shoe." The other grown-ups there—not quite behaving like grown-ups—were Kipling's father ("the Pater") and a family doctor. They seem to have worried about possibly toxic lead paint on the brightly colored animals, hence the sucking on the toy cows.

A toy Noah's Ark much like Josephine's appears in Kipling's devastating early story "Baa Baa, Black Sheep." The story was widely assumed to be fictional (although Aunt Louie would have known the truth) until the posthumous publication of Kipling's autobiography, *Something of Myself.* There, Kipling makes clear that "Baa Baa, Black Sheep" is a lightly disguised account of the abuse he suffered when he and his sister, Trix, were abandoned for five and a half years to the care of a cruel guardian while their parents returned to India. "The real tragedy sprang from our inability to understand why our parents had deserted us," Trix wrote of the ordeal. "It was like a double death, or rather like an avalanche that had swept away everything happy and familiar." Their mother, informed that little Rudyard was showing alarming symptoms we would now characterize as psychotic, eventually showed up to retrieve him. "She told me afterward," he remembered, "that when she first came up to my room to kiss me good-night, I flung up an arm to guard off the cuff that I had been trained to expect."

"Baa Baa, Black Sheep" ends with the rescue of the abused children, called Punch (or, alternatively, Black Sheep) and Judy. The little boy assures his sister that "we are just as much Mother's as if she had never gone." But the closing lines tell a different, darker story: "Not altogether... for when young lips have drunk deep of the bitter waters of Hate, Suspicion, and Despair, all the Love in the world will not wholly take away that knowledge, though it may turn darkened eyes for a while to the light." At the lowest emotional point in the story, abandoned and desperate, Black Sheep decides to kill himself. "A knife would hurt," he reflects, "but Aunty Rosa had told him, a year ago, that if he sucked paint he would die. He went into the nursery, unearthed the now disused Noah's Ark and sucked the paint off as many animals as remained. It tasted abominable, but he had licked Noah's Dove clean by the time Aunty Rosa and Judy returned." He doesn't die, however. "It may be, that the makers of Noah's Arks know that their animals are likely to find their way into young mouths, and paint them accordingly."

Kipling mentions no suicide attempt in *Something of Myself*. Did the episode with the Noah's Ark toy actually happen? The question, unanswerable, is less significant than Kipling's imaginative use of the Ark. When Punch licks the paint clean from Noah's dove, he is about to be rescued, Noah-like, from the scene of disaster—by his mother, as it happens. Literally ingesting the paint suggests two infantile connections to the lost mother: the comfort of nursing and, alternatively, of licking the plate clean. The detail of how Kipling, now a father, "sucked a red and white moo-cow hard" confirms the association with nursing.

4.

Kipling drew his own illustrations for *Just So Stories*, another gift for Josephine. These remarkable drawings have a proto-Surrealist energy, combining dream motifs, children's impressions, and hyper-close attention to observed detail. He signed them with an enigmatic artist's seal, or maker's mark. The first time the seal appeared, below an illustration for "How the Camel Got His Hump," it seemed part of the scenery of the "world so new and all" in which the tale was set. The seal consisted of a small Noah's Ark perched on a live volcano, with a trail of smoke passing over its roof. This odd image evolved from one illustration to the next, until it morphed into a capital *A* (the volcano with the line of smoke across it) enclosing a boat. The correct reading of this rebus was that the boat was a Noah's Ark placed under an *A*: hence, *Ark + A*, to be pronounced "RK." Kipling's letter *A* also resembled the gateway, or *torii*, to a Japanese shrine. "Everyone knows what a *torii* is," Kipling wrote in one of his travel letters from Japan. "They have them in Southern India. A great King makes a note of the place where he intends to build a huge arch, but being a King, does so in stone, not ink." Not being a king, Kipling sketched his own arch, or ark, in ink.

Kipling never explained what the *Ark + A* insignia meant. In fact, he seemed at pains to suppress any such speculation. "The Elephant's Child" is a parable of education, in which the young elephant, burdened with "satiable curtiosity," learns about the dangers of the world and is rewarded for it by his useful trunk. On the following page an illustration of the elephant having its nose pulled by a crocodile, Kipling added an ornamental border and a caption. "Underneath the truly picture are shadows of African animals walking into an African ark," he explained. "There are two lions, two ostriches, two oxen, two camels, two sheep, and two other things that look like rats, but I think they are rock-rabbits. They don't mean anything," he added. "I put them in because I thought they looked pretty."

A rebus involving an Ark and the letter *A* is not a self-evident choice for the initials *RK*. It is, in some obvious sense, *reached for*. And it would seem to involve at least a double—and perhaps triple—emphasis on beginnings. *A* is the first letter of the alphabet (a subsequent *Just So* story will explain the origins of the alphabet), while the Ark signifies a new

How the elephant got his trunk.

beginning on a newly consecrated earth. Kipling may also be alluding to the Greek word *arche*, as in archeology, which also means "beginning."

5.

Meanwhile, Rudyard and Carrie, long confined to tiny Bliss Cottage, were envisioning a dream house for their family. The plan for the house resembled a houseboat perched on the hillside like Noah's Ark on Ararat. The house, to be called Naulakha in honor of Wolcott Balestier, would meld memories of India with Kipling's fresh sense of Vermont. Ninety feet long and a mere thirty feet wide, the width of a single room, the house, as Kipling conceived it, would appear to be "riding on its hillside like a little boat on the flank of a far wave." Kipling consulted with the designer Lockwood de Forest, a friend of his father's, who may have suggested an analogy with the narrow houseboats of Kashmir. On his visit to New York in 1889, Kipling had been enthralled with de Forest's Indian-style town house on East Tenth Street, with its entryway of carved teak. For Naulakha, de Forest gave the Kiplings an Indian sideboard for the dining room, with carved teak panels that suggested the doorways and porticoes of a luxurious bungalow.

Many of the ideas for the house came from Kipling himself, but he needed a sympathetic architect to realize them. He was fortunate to have Henry Rutgers Marshall, a student of the great American architect H. H. Richardson, as his creative partner. "Marshall Sahib is coming to see us early in September I believe," Kipling wrote Meta de Forest in mid-August. "He will sit on our site and tell us about the house." A Columbia College classmate of de Forest, Marshall happened to be a prominent psychologist as well as an architect. What he had to say about Naulakha can be surmised from the book, *Pain, Pleasure, and Aesthetics,* that he was completing as he drew up the plans. Published in 1894 and judged "almost 'epoch-making'" by William James, the book was based on an ingenious theory of the emotions. Pleasure, in Marshall's view, resulted from efficient response to stimuli, while pain derived from inefficient response. For Marshall, the history of art was a progressive "elimination of the ugly," those inefficient barriers to pleasure. In architecture, he wrote, "Each new work has made it possible to eliminate some form, which had been displeasing in the last effort, to alter some unsatisfactory surface, to change some deficient shadow depth."

What this meant in practice was an architecture of radical simplicity. Marshall had come closest to his ideals in his majestic design for the First Presbyterian Church in Colorado Springs. With its expanses of native rock and its line of great pillars, the church radiates a western embrace of the outdoors. Just as Henry Adams had given Richardson an opportunity to experiment with Japanese simplicity—what Frank Lloyd Wright called "elimination of the insignificant"—in his home opposite the White House on Lafayette Square, Kipling gave Marshall a chance

Naulakha, photograph by Neal Rantoul.

to experiment with his own pared-down aesthetic. Naulakha, a house named in memory of a beloved friend and brother, was, to borrow Marshall's own schema, a house to assuage pain. In this regard, it resembles the Wish House in one of Kipling's greatest stories, in which clients visit a haunted house to alleviate the pain of loved ones by assuming it themselves.

The house perched on the Vermont hillside had healing powers for others as well. A favorite jaunt for Rudyard and Carrie was to drive their horse and carriage across the Connecticut River, from the Brattleboro side to the flanks of Wantastiquet, their "guardian mountain" on the New Hampshire side. On one such excursion, they approached a remote farmhouse and were welcomed by a "wild-eyed" woman who asked fiercely "Be you the new lights 'crost the valley yonder? Ye don't know what a comfort they've been to me this winter. Ye aren't ever going to shroud 'em up—or *be* ye?" Kipling assured her that they had no such plans. "So, as long as we lived there, that broad side of 'Naulakha' which looked her-ward was always nakedly lit."

6.

As he acquainted himself with his new surroundings, Kipling discovered that Brattleboro was a safe refuge for other people as well. He would drive into Brattleboro by carriage or sleigh, depending on the weather, to pick up his mail or to have a convivial chat with locals in the basement bar of the Brooks House on Main Street. Notched at the confluence of two rivers, the mighty Connecticut and the smaller West River, Brattleboro had two distinct faces. It was a market town for the region, the hub for encircling farms and forests. The country people drove their horse-drawn wagons into town on Tuesdays to sell their squash and tomatoes, and stopped by the pharmacy for their medications. On Sundays they came again, scrubbed and laundered, to attend the churches downtown. Pious Brattleboro was officially dry, but homemade liquor was easy to come by. "One found in almost every office the water-bottle and thick tooth-glass displayed openly, and in discreet cupboards or drawers the whisky bottle," Kipling noted. Men drank hard cider on the farms, achieving "almost maniacal forms of drunkenness."

Brattleboro was also a refuge for summer people. Southerners were drawn to its mild climate. Visitors from Boston and New York came back regularly like migrating birds and began building fanciful second homes—quaint Elizabethan cottages and sumptuous Queen Annes—on the so-called terraces, which ascended like forested stairways from the river. Summer people enjoyed the town's musical life—Brattleboro boasted a famous organ factory—and the lovely carriage rides up into the surrounding hills and farms. It was easy to feel, in the tree-lined streets and terraces, that the stern dictates of the Puritan religion, which had mushroomed up the Connecticut River, were on the wane. "It is strange to me," wrote the novelist Fanny Fern, a regular visitor, "that everyone doesn't live in Brattleboro."

Three audacious experiments in achieving perfection in *this* world gave to the village of Brattleboro a distinctive quality, a peculiar flavor, unmatched by other New England towns. All three experiments took root in the 1840s, finding inspiration in the healing powers of nature. One experiment was an innovative asylum for the mentally ill, the Brattleboro Retreat, founded on the belief that mental health was best achieved through communion with nature and through creative activities such as handicrafts and music. A second experiment was the Putney perfectionist community, founded by Brattleboro native John Humphrey Noyes. Contrary to Calvinist tenets, Noyes believed that freedom from sin could be achieved in this world. What he called "exclusive marriage" brought nothing but unhappiness, he claimed, and he based his community on "free love" (a phrase he coined) and the sharing of sexual partners. Hounded from Putney, just up the road from Naulakha, by legal authorities, Noyes moved his operation to Oneida, New York, where his followers made silver-plate flatware for American tables.

The third experiment was a luxury hotel devoted to the curative properties of fresh water. The Wesselhoeft Water Cure originated in an act of political violence in Germany. In 1819, a student named Karl Ludwig Sand paid an unannounced visit to the popular German dramatist August von Kotzebue, a political conservative, in his comfortable home in Mannheim. Sand drew a dagger from his sleeve and stabbed Kotzebue in the breast. The first political assassination in modern German history had wide-ranging repercussions. It brought German philosophy to Emerson's Concord circle. It also, indirectly, brought Rudyard Kipling to Brattleboro.

Sand had been a member of the students' union in Jena. This circle, under the charismatic leadership of a poet named Karl Follen, was committed to revolutionary German nationalism. In the immediate aftermath of the Kotzebue murder, Count Metternich's secret police rounded up students, professors, and journalists. Among these was Follen himself, who escaped to the United States, taking up a new career teaching German at Harvard. Follen served as a conduit of German culture to

Emerson's transcendentalist circle, inspiring a new reverence for the natural world.

Another man caught up in Metternich's dragnet was a young medical student named Robert Wesselhoeft. After serving seven years in prison, he followed Follen to America and opened a medical practice in Cambridge. Wesselhoeft, who had been introduced to the so-called "water cure" by its founder, Vincenz Pressnitz, practiced both hydrotherapy and homeopathy, and opened a water cure establishment in West Roxbury, outside Boston. Patients undergoing the cure were awakened at dawn, wrapped in towels until they perspired, and dipped in cold water to cleanse their pores. They drank only water—coffee, tea, and alcohol were strictly forbidden—and took long walks in the countryside.

The prominent writer and physician Dr. Oliver Wendell Holmes delivered a pair of lectures in 1842 in which he denounced the "pretended science" of homeopathy. Wesselhoeft was Holmes's principal target, one of those dangerous quacks who, according to Holmes, "announce themselves ready to relinquish all the accumulated treasure of our art, to trifle with life upon the strength of these fantastic theories." Holmes's much-noticed attack on Wesselhoeft had interesting repercussions for American literature. Hawthorne based a character in his novel *The Blithedale Romance* on Wesselhoeft (renamed Westervelt). Finding Cambridge intolerable after Holmes's attack, Wesselhoeft fled to Brattleboro, where he established his water cure, in the process transforming the sleepy village into a fashionable resort.

To the Wesselhoeft Water Cure came the famous and the once famous. A long list of visitors, documented by Kipling's friend Molly Cabot, recalls Gatsby's party guests. Longfellow came to take the waters. So did William Dean Howells and writer Helen Hunt Jackson. And so did "Doctor Kane, the Arctic explorer," whose name was "carved on the trunk of a mighty pine." One Charles O. Simpson came "year after year," and "gave the name Staubbach, after the famous German waterfall, to the nearly perpendicular drop of sixty feet, where the water of

Fall Brook on its way to West River, beyond West Dummerston, runs over an abrupt ledge of rock." After the Civil War came Generals George McClellan and William Tecumseh Sherman. And finally, there were those who became permanent residents, among them "Mr. and Mrs. Joseph N. Balestier." And thus, it was the water cure that first brought Carrie Balestier's family to Brattleboro, indirectly bringing Rudyard Kipling there as well.

7.

Soon enough, Naulakha itself became a destination for pilgrims, especially literary ones, eager to pay their respects to Kipling at his hillside refuge. The poet Bliss Carman, known for his songs of a vagabond, arrived, and wrote a sonnet to Kipling that began, "What need have you of praising?" Owen Wister, author of *The Virginian,* came, too. And so did Frank Doubleday, a young publisher eager to corner the market on Kipling's works in the United States. Another visitor was Arthur Conan Doyle, who arrived at Naulakha in November 1894. Creator of Sherlock Holmes and a former client of Wolcott Balestier's, Conan Doyle was invited to Beatty's house for Thanksgiving dinner. "No man," Balestier quipped, "would want to keep Thanksgiving in an Englishman's house." Conan Doyle was on a lecture tour in support of good relations between Britain and the United States. He brought along his golf clubs, and the two writers enthusiastically swatted their balls around the meadows while puzzled neighbors looked on at the unfamiliar game. Kipling and Conan Doyle talked and smoked on the Naulakha veranda, sharing stories about their interest in telepathy and the paranormal, a passion of Conan Doyle's and the subject of Kipling's *The Finest Story in the World.*

The visit from Conan Doyle activated yet another aspect of Kipling's fixation on Noah's Ark. Conan Doyle was a Freemason, and so, as it happened, was Kipling, who had joined the half-secret organization, inspired by medieval guilds of craftsmen, during his early years in India. Conan Doyle's visit inspired a poem in which Kipling fondly remembered his own initiation in 1886, when he was twenty years old, into the Masonic Lodge in Lahore, his "Mother Lodge." In Kipling's dialect poem, caste, religion, and social status were left at the door: "Outside—'Sergeant! Sir! Salute! Salaam!' / Inside—'Brother,' an' it doesn't do no 'arm." "Here I met Muslims, Hindus, Sikhs, members of the Araya and Brahmo Samaj," Kipling later recalled, "and a Jew tyler [an official position in the Lodge], who was priest and butcher to his little community in the city."

For Kipling, Masonry provided a map of occult symbols against which he plotted his life and work. It was the only church that Kipling believed in ("I haven't much religion," says a character in his story "In the Interests of the Brethren," "but all I had I learnt in Lodge"), and it inspired many of his writings, from the emphasis on personal responsibility in *The Jungle Book*—prompted, Kipling claimed, by "some memory of the Masonic Lions" in a children's magazine—to the extraordinary tale "The Janeites," in which a group of British soldiers on the front, all Masons, form a secret organization based on the arcana of Jane Austen novels.

There are degrees in Freemasonry, and on April 14, 1887, Kipling was promoted to the rank of Royal Ark Mariner, with the Mount Ararat Mariners Lodge No. 98 in Lahore. The Royal Ark is closely allied to the Mark degree, which Kipling received the same day, and which also employs the symbolism of Noah's Ark. Kipling's elevation to the status of Royal Ark Mariner coincided with the writing of "Baa Baa, Black Sheep," with its toy Noah's Ark, and "The Man Who Would Be King," his parable of imperial overreach, which employs Masonic ritual. It also reinforced the importance of Noah's Ark as his own private symbol.

Kipling's personal rebus of an Ark and a capital *A* is easily solved. The puzzle of his larger self-identification with the story of Noah's Ark is more complicated. As a very young boy, Kipling suffered the fate that every child fears most: that of being abandoned, without explanation or hope of rescue, by his parents. Placed in the hands of abusive strangers, he decided, perhaps, that his only recourse was to kill himself. When his mother finally returned, he felt relief, but his outlook on the world was forever darkened by this early betrayal.

Kipling's writing, early and late, seeks to establish a zone of safety in a precarious world, enlisting three different phases of the biblical figure of Noah. Noah as Survivor presides over the earliest phase of Kipling's life, as documented in "Baa Baa, Black Sheep." Noah as Father informs his relations with Josephine. And Noah as Builder guides the design of Naulakha, his Ark on the Vermont hillside. It is tempting to find Noah's Ark lurking everywhere in Kipling's life, a Rosetta Stone that translates his life and work into some coherent pattern. Of course, no human life, especially one as complicated as Rudyard Kipling's, can be reduced to one overriding pattern or to a single symbol. And yet the story of Noah's Ark and the dove's good news remained a promise of protection for Kipling, in an unpredictable world that sometimes violated such promises.

Chapter Six

———

THE FOURTH DIMENSION

I.

During the summer of 1893, Lockwood Kipling arrived in Vermont for
an extended visit and admired the progress on Naulakha. Before returning to England, he added a finishing touch to his son's study at the south
end of the house. With plaster letters over the mantelpiece, he inscribed
the words "The night cometh, when no man can work." Both of Rudyard's grandfathers were Methodist preachers, but his parents were not
religious by temperament. "The hair of the dog," his mother, Alice, once
remarked, as she consigned a lock of hair from Methodism's founder,
John Wesley, to the fire. But the family revered the King James Bible.
The full quotation from the Gospel of John ("I must work the works of
him that sent me, while it is day: the night cometh, when no man can
work") is customarily shortened by clipping the ending and abbreviating
what comes before, thus yielding the upbeat message, "Work while it is

day." Kipling's next book of stories, conceived in Vermont, was titled *The Day's Work.*

And yet Lockwood's decision to emphasize the dark side—the *night* side—of the admonition is oddly fitting in Rudyard's case. *The Day's Work* includes several stories that might better be called *The Night's Work,* since they explore what Kipling came to think of as the Fourth Dimension, the darker region of experience accessible by means of drugs, dreams, and hallucinations. The title of Kipling's story "An Error in the Fourth Dimension" alludes to this realm of the unknown, the night world. It is about an American millionaire who settles in the English countryside only to find that he is adrift amid the local customs. The story, Kipling explained to a correspondent, was about the hidden dimension in every country, "in which no one except a lawful native of the land can move without violent collisions."

To gain access to this Fourth Dimension required a violence of a different kind, what the poet Rimbaud described as a "systematic derangement of the senses." Despite his reputation as a guardian of traditional values, Kipling was willing to risk physical and psychological side effects in order to reach the Fourth Dimension. And as he continued to explore his own newly adopted country, the United States, he found himself imaginatively reliving, in stories like "The Bridge-Builders," how he had first gained access to what he had come to consider the real India. What had given him such access was opium.

2.

On a May morning in 1893, Kipling drove his horse-drawn carriage into Brattleboro to pick up the mail, abundant as usual, and found a letter from his uncle Alfred. Alfred Baldwin was a Conservative member of Parliament, and he had a puzzling request for his nephew. Parliament, he explained, had taken up the thorny political issue of opium. The

British Empire had fought two cynical wars, the shameful Opium Wars, to maintain the Chinese market for Indian opium, a hugely lucrative export. It could even be said that the British Empire had been founded on the opium trade. And yet there was mounting resistance in England, spearheaded by Quakers and other activists, to opium production, along with increasingly strenuous efforts in Parliament to hasten its abolition. Baldwin wanted an insider's opinion of the matter, and he thought he knew just the man to ask. His nephew had, after all, written several early stories about opium use, including the widely admired "The Gate of the Hundred Sorrows."

Kipling did not disappoint. During his seven years in India, he told his uncle, he had been responsible for some fifty servants, all from "the class most notoriously addicted to drugs." Only one of these had regularly drugged himself "insensible." Moderation was the overriding pattern. "The native of India is by nature and environment temperate," Kipling maintained, "and his dealings with the drug (an excellent thing in itself and in moderation about as harmful as tobacco) are most strictly limited." He concluded with a dig at the anti-opium faction in England and the writers enlisted to make the case. "The 'opium den' as described in the highly colored fiction of the Cause does not exist."

Uncle Alfred was not the only prominent person to seek Kipling's opinion about opium during his Vermont sojourn. On one of his periodic visits to New York, Kipling was engaged in conversation at the Authors' Club by Dr. Robert Dawbarn, a professor of surgery at City Hospital. Dawbarn asked what Kipling thought of opium. "Naturally, from the author of 'The Gate of a Hundred Sorrows,' I expected a scathing denunciation of the drug," Dawbarn reported in a medical journal. "Instead, Kipling spoke of it as the friend, and in certain ways the mainstay of millions there among the natives."

Kipling proceeded to denounce the "mote-and-beam" hypocrisy of English clergymen who, after a short vacation in India, would "preach rancorously against the opium traffic in India" and its peaceful users, while "overlooking the crying home evil of drunken and quarrelsome men, women, and children upon the streets of every English town." Kipling insisted on the medical benefits of opium as a treatment for malaria. He claimed "as an indisputable fact" that regular users of opium in India "are strengthened thereby for arduous labors." He concluded with the warning note that while native users only indulged up to a certain point, "the white habitué of opium generally does not stop," steadily upping the dosage "until a wrecked life is the result."

These surprising exchanges hint at Kipling's own experience with the drug, as an aid to "arduous labors." They also provide the context for one of Kipling's greatest stories. In "The Bridge-Builders," written in Naulakha and published at the end of 1893, Kipling memorialized his own first experience of opium, when a servant prepared a pipe for him during a midnight crisis. The story also registered his experience in Vermont as a builder of a complicated new house. Lockwood Kipling visited Brattleboro just in time to help his son with both the interior design of his new house and with the architecture of one of his most complex stories.

3.

Kipling first took opium—or the "black smoke," as it was known—in September 1884, when he was eighteen. As a newspaper editor and reporter in Lahore, he was impatient to embark on his real career as a writer of fiction and verse. His family was in Simla, the summer refuge for colonial officials, in the cooler mountains. He himself had endured, alone, a hot and difficult summer. A fever had brought on the kind of visual disorders and hallucinations that he had previously experienced during his difficult years with a foster family in England. On September 16, in the middle of the night, his symptoms suddenly intensified, and he writhed on the floor in pain. His manservant, Kadir Baksh, fled from the house. Desperate, Kipling poured himself "a pretty stiff dose of chloro-dyne," apparently unaware that the medication consisted of opium dis-solved in a solution of alcohol, along with cannabis and chloroform.

Baksh returned with an oil lamp, a small bottle, and "a queer looking weapon." The weapon turned out to be a pipe, along with several opium pills, and Baksh insisted that his master smoke as much as he could. "Presently I felt the cramps in my legs dying out and my tummy more settled," Kipling wrote, "and a minute or two later it seemed to me that I fell through the floor." This double dose of opium was the only time that Kipling publicly acknowledged taking drugs, although his letters indicate, as Charles Allen notes, that "he continued to rely on opiates, in the form of opium, morphine and *bhang* or Indian hemp medicinally taken, to get him through Lahore's hot summer nights."

But opiates served Kipling in a more significant way than merely al-leviating pain or insomnia. He discovered that night, not day, brought the most promise for the kind of work that interested him. His job as news-paper reporter gave him access to places barred to other Europeans. "Having no position to consider, and my trade enforcing it, I could move at will in the Fourth Dimension," Kipling wrote in *Something of Myself* of his nocturnal prowls in Lahore. "Often the night got into my head . . . and I would wander till dawn in all manner of odd places—liquor-shops, gambling and opium-dens . . . or in and about the narrow gullies under the Mosque of Wazir Khan for the sheer sake of looking." He concluded, "Much of real Indian life goes on in the hot weather nights."

Soon, Kipling was ready to display the triumphant results of his night's work. Ten days after his opium binge, his short story "The Gate of the Hundred Sorrows" appeared in the *Civil and Military Gazette*. It was the first story written for his landmark collection *Plain Tales from the Hills* and marks the true beginning of Kipling's career as a fiction writer. The opium den that serves as its setting is among those narrow gullies that Kipling explored at night: "It lies between the Coppersmith's Gully and the pipe-stem sellers' quarter, within a hundred yards, too, as the crow flies, of the Mosque of Wazir Khan." The challenge facing Kipling was to give believable voice to an addict sinking to his inevitable end. When he revised the newspaper version for *Plain Tales*, Kipling appended a frame narrative in which we are told that the events were recounted "between moonset and morning," a few weeks before the doomed opium user died.

The opium den is a house rather than a gate, and is all but invisible. "You might even go through the very gully it stands in a hundred times, and be none the wiser." It first belonged to a Chinese man whose coffin, "lacquered black, with red and gold writings on it," is a conspicuous feature of the house. The speaker, a Eurasian named Gabral Misquitta, identifies three phases of his descent into opium addiction. "How did I take to it?" he asks rhetorically. "I used to try it in my own house, just to see what it was like." Then he found his way to the gully. "It was a *pukka*, respectable opium-house," he insists, with "clean mats and pillows, and the best stuff you could get anywhere."

Soon, he was hooked, and here Kipling shows off his insider's knowledge of opium use. He vividly portrays, with a relish that recalls his passion for Whitman's poetry, the multiethnic character of the clientele—"two Babus [educated Indians] from a Government Office . . . a half-caste woman, and a couple of men who said they had come from the North . . . Persians or Afghans or something"—but his main distinction is between white people and the rest. "Nothing grows on you so much, if you're white, as the Black Smoke," Misquitta notes of his five years of addiction. The establishment has declined, in his view, now that the old man's nephew has assumed control. The nephew favors "cheap stuff" over the high-quality opium provided by his uncle. "I've found burnt bran in my pipe over and over again." Interestingly, Kipling makes little attempt to describe the physical or psychological effects of opium use, other than the visual illusion that the red and black dragons on the coffin seem to writhe under its influence.

4.

If opium was the subject of Kipling's first story, it was also at the heart of his first serious attempt at writing a novel. "The idea of 'Mother Maturin' dawned on me today," he wrote in his diary on March 7, 1885, a few months after the publication of "The Gate of the Hundred Sorrows." By July, he informed his aunt Edith that the novel had grown "like Topsy," a playful reference, drawn from a character in *Uncle Tom's Cabin,* to family friend William Morris's expansive girth. "It's not one bit nice or proper but it carries a grim sort of a moral with it and tries to deal with the unutterable horrors of a lower-class Eurasian and native life as they exist outside the reports." He had shown the draft to his sister, who found it "awfully horrid," and to his mother, who pronounced it "nasty but powerful." But the fullest account comes from Kipling's American friend Ted Hill, who described it as "the story of an old Irish woman who kept an opium den in Lahore but sent her daughter to be educated in England. She marries a civilian and comes to live in Lahore—hence a story—how Govt. Secrets came to be known in the bazar and vice versa."

We are clearly in Zola territory here, the lowlife realm of naturalism. The French name of the heroine suggests an affiliation with Zola's novels of prostitution, alcoholism, and degradation, which Kipling had studied assiduously, even noting, in one of his atmospheric accounts of a typical night prowl in Lahore, titled "The City of Dreadful Night," how only Zola could do it justice. Such "experiments in misery," as Kipling's American disciple Stephen Crane called excursions to see how the poor and the marginalized really lived, became a staple of the next generation of writers inspired by Kipling. These writers sought to demonstrate—with a nod to Darwin—how environmental circumstance determines the evolution of character.

Kipling never published "Mother Maturin," and the manuscript has vanished. But it remains a striking fact that his first published story and his first serious attempt at a novel were both inspired in part by opium. Moreover, readers of *Kim* will recognize the survival, in one of Kipling's greatest works, of some of the narrative threads mentioned by Ted Hill. For Kim, too, is raised by a woman who uses opium, as does his Irish father. And the secrets that the mercurial Kim, as a government spy for the British, traffics in were precisely of the Fourth Dimension kind that "came to be known in the bazar."

5.

Kipling had been using opium and its derivatives for four years when, in January 1888, he interrupted a railroad journey from Allahabad to Calcutta in order to learn more about the drug. He made arrangements to visit the opium factory on the banks of the Ganges River, in the city of Ghazipur, where a family friend held the lucrative sinecure as opium agent. Downstream from Benares (Varanasi), Ghazipur was one of two locations with huge factories—the other was in Patna—that maintained the Indian government monopoly on opium production. The drug had become an increasingly valuable export commodity, principally to China, since the Revolt of 1857, when Britain tightened its hold on the Indian economy after the native challenge to its rule. The Ghazipur factory remains, to this day, the largest opium production plant in the world.

From its opening sentence, Kipling's article "In an Opium Factory" emphasizes the value and scale of this cash crop. "On the banks of the Ganges, forty miles below Benares as the crow flies, stands the Ghazipur Factory, an opium mint as it were, whence issue the precious cakes that are to replenish the coffers of the Indian Government." Everyone who handles the raw material, Kipling notes, treats it "as though it were gold." Making opium is an art, Kipling insists, as he describes each painstaking step of its manufacture. Despite its characterization as factory-made, there is nothing mechanical about opium production. A skilled worker "tucks in the top of the cone with his hands, brings the fringe of cake over to close the opening, and pastes fresh leaves upon all." Kipling assumes the point of view of a connoisseur, and possibly consumer. "That is the drug the Chinaman likes."

6.

In Kipling's great story "The Bridge-Builders," written at Naulakha in 1893, access to the real India is again granted by opium. The opening story in Kipling's Vermont collection *The Day's Work*, "The Bridge-Builders" is Kipling's authoritative statement about the precarious balance between the claims of the day's work and the counterclaims of the night and the Fourth Dimension. The British-born engineer Findlayson has been working for three years on a railway bridge spanning the Ganges. The bridge stood "before him in the sunlight, lacking only a few weeks' work on the girders of the three middle piers—his bridge, raw and ugly as original sin, but *pukka*, permanent."

But those remaining weeks open the way for disaster. Although it is not yet flood season, urgent reports reach Findlayson that the waters of the Ganges are rising. He and his crew work deep into the night to secure building materials, tools, and the bridge itself against the inexorably rising water. "The order in all cases was to stand by the day's work and wait instructions." As dusk descends, "the riveters began a night's work, racing against the flood that was to come." Such is the desperate rhythm Kipling establishes, as the day's work alternates with the night's.

Findlayson's native foreman, Peroo, is at his side during these feverish preparations. A former sailor, Peroo has come to revere the technical expertise of his employers. When he first entered the engine room of a steamship, we are told, "he prayed to the low-pressure cylinder." His response anticipates the famous remark of Henry Adams, contemplating dynamos at the world's fair of 1900: "Before the end, one began to pray to it; inherited instinct taught the natural expression of man before silent and infinite force." Peroo is the kind of loyal native Kipling most admires, a cosmopolitan traveler and jack-of-all-trades who nonetheless submits to the authority of his European masters.

But Peroo also retains native beliefs and practices. Troubled by Findlayson's refusal to rest as the flood rises, Peroo slips his master a tobacco box and urges him to partake. "It is no more than opium," he says reassuringly, "clean Malwa opium!" Findlayson shakes a few brownish pellets into his hand and swallows them absentmindedly. "The stuff was at least a good guard against fever," he reflects, "the fever that was creeping upon him out of the wet mud—and he had seen what Peroo could do in the stewing mists of Autumn on the strength of a dose from the tin box." The scene is both a reenactment of Kipling's own first experience with opium, when he was a reporter in Lahore, and a restatement of his claims to Dr. Dawbarn in New York, regarding the drug's efficacy against malaria and in support of "arduous labors."

As the boat Peroo has secured for his safety spins dizzily out of control, so does Findlayson's opium-addled mind. Trying to focus on one of the supporting piers, he can't settle his impressions. "The figures would not shape themselves to the eye except one by one and at enormous intervals of time. There was a sound rich and mellow in his ears like the deepest note of a double bass—an entrancing sound upon which he pondered for several hours, as it seemed." Asked if he can swim, he assures Peroo that he can fly instead, "fly as swiftly as the wind." Findlayson's response to his drug-induced psychosis is to take still more opium, "staring through the mist at the nothing that was there," a phrase strangely reminiscent of Wallace Stevens's line, in "The Snow Man," "Nothing that is not there and the nothing that is."

The biblical language resumes, regarding what is now referred to, with a capital letter, as "the Flood," but in a different verbal register, a kind of drug-induced magical realism. "In his mind, Findlayson had already escaped from the boat, and was circling high in air to find a rest for the sole of his foot." The allusion is to Noah's first attempt to see if the waters had sufficiently receded for the inhabitants of the Ark to disembark safely. He sends forth a dove. "But the dove found no rest for the sole of her foot, and she returned unto him into the ark, for the waters were on the face of the whole earth." Noah was a builder, too, but Findlayson, spinning down the river toward an abandoned island, is sure that his bridge is long gone: "the Deluge had swept it away, leaving this one island under heaven for Findlayson and his companion, sole survivors of the breed of Man."

7.

Nothing in Findlayson's previous hallucinations prepares the reader for what happens next, as the spinning Ark finally runs aground on its Ararat in the Ganges. One by one, to the amazement of the stranded mariners, the native Hindu gods of India appear, in the guise of their "vehicles," their beasts of burden: first the Bull, Brahma himself; then Kali and Shiva; and finally the monkey god, Hanuman. The deities gather to listen to Mother Gunga's complaints. She, the Ganges River, pleads for revenge against the intrusive bridge builders, who have imprisoned her waters with their modern technology. "I have seen Sydney," Peroo tells Findlayson. "I have seen London, and twenty great ports, but . . . never man has seen that we saw here." Findlayson either doesn't understand what Peroo is saying or he refuses to do so. But Peroo persists. "Has the Sahib forgotten; or do we black men only see the Gods?" "There was a fever upon me," Findlayson answers uneasily, looking across the water. "It seemed that the island was full of beasts and men talking, but I do not remember."

The ending of the story may seem the rankest orientalism, a sentimental view of native superstitions, based in part on Lockwood Kipling's loving account in his book *Beast and Man in India*. The Hindus have their gods of the night, of the deep, unchanging past. The Europeans, by contrast, have their progressive gods of technology, the low-pressure cylinder. The natives are Nature and the past; the Europeans are Science and the future. Only black men see the gods. As Kipling noted, in an 1885 letter to his cousin Margaret Burne-Jones, "Underneath our excellent administrative system; under the piles of reports and statistics; the thousands of troops; the doctors; and the civilians runs wholly untouched and unaffected the life of the people of the land—a life as full of impossibilities and wonders as the Arabian nights."

But this hierarchy is too simple for Kipling, at least in "The Bridge-Builders." His Hindu gods do not present a unified vision; they energetically disagree among themselves. Mother Gunga does indeed lobby hard for the rights of Nature, the timeless cycle of flood and drought. But Hanuman, who seems to have drifted to India from the modern industrial world (and perhaps from some city near Brattleboro, Vermont), speaks for technology. "I have made a man worship the fire-carriage as it stood still breathing smoke, and he knew not that he worshipped me." Hanuman is the voice of materialism, of the railroad engineers, and the bridge builders in their daytime work.

Only Peroo, in this commanding story, seems to have achieved a proper balance between the claims of the night and the day. Only he remembers, in the sunlit day, what he has seen on the island at night. Findlayson has built one kind of bridge, the daytime bridge over the Ganges. It is Findlayson who is the hero of the first part of the story; we, the readers, experience progress on the monumental bridge from his point of view. But Peroo has bridged something else entirely, something that, ultimately, is more important for Kipling, writing in Vermont in 1893, and discussing the gods of India with his father, Lockwood. Peroo understands the claims of both kinds of gods, the gods of the daytime and—with the help of opium—the gods of the night. It is Peroo's perspective that, in Kipling's scheme, takes over for the ending. It is Peroo who, at the end of a long day's night of work, has had his vision. Meanwhile, Kipling, holed up in his study at the south end of Naulakha, stared at his father's injunction in the flickering candlelight, "The night cometh, when no man can work," and went on writing anyway. Opium had opened some of the mysteries of India to Kipling, but what wondrous drug could reveal the hidden Fourth Dimension of the United States?

Chapter Seven

———

ADOPTED BY WOLVES

I.

Kipling's first achievement in *The Jungle Book* is to establish, from its opening words, a believable family of wolves, neither overly anthropomorphic nor too alien and wild:

> It was seven o'clock of a very warm evening in the Seeonee hills when Father Wolf woke up from his day's rest, scratched himself, yawned, and spread out his paws one after the other to get rid of the sleepy feeling in their tips. Mother Wolf lay with her big gray nose dropped across her four tumbling, squealing cubs, and the moon shone into the mouth of the cave where they all lived. "Augrh!" said Father Wolf. "It is time to hunt again."

When Kipling specifies how Father Wolf spreads out his paws, one after the other, to get rid of the sleepy feeling in their tips, he turns us all into wolves.

Into this cozy domestic scene a tiny stranger intrudes. Father Wolf identifies the visitor as "a man's cub," separated from his terrified parents by the marauding tiger, Shere Khan. Mother Wolf, meanwhile, is nursing her own cubs. "How little! How naked, and—how bold!" she remarks. Her last observation coincides with the man cub's efforts to muscle his way among the wolf cubs and get some milk for himself. "The baby was pushing his way between the cubs to get close to the warm hide," Kipling writes. "Ahai!" says Mother Wolf. "He is taking his meal with the others.... Now, was there ever a wolf that could boast of a man's cub among her children?" This is meant as a rhetorical question, but Father Wolf answers it anyway: "I have heard now and again of such a thing," he says, "but never in our Pack or in my time."

Most readers (or viewers of the classic 1967 Disney adaptation) are familiar with Mowgli's progress among his wolf brothers; his tutelage under the kindly bear, Baloo, as he learns the precepts of the Law of the Jungle; the teachings of more severe panther, Bagheera, who was born in captivity and knows the ways of men; his ambiguous relations with the deadly snake, Kaa; his fight-to-the-death hostility toward the tiger, Shere Khan. These are all part of our mythology, as enduring as Huck Finn or Tarzan, that latter-day Mowgli. We come to accept Mowgli's wolf family as his real family, his primary allegiance. "I have obeyed the Law of the Jungle, and there is no wolf of ours from whose paws I have not pulled a thorn," Mowgli says. "Surely they are my brothers!" We allow ourselves to be outraged, later in the book, when he is kidnapped by a band of monkeys, as though wolves are closer in nature to humans than monkeys are. We might contrast this upbringing with that of Tarzan, who is adopted by humanoid apes, a much closer link in the evolutionary chain, as Edgar Rice Burroughs repeatedly reminds us.

No moment in *The Jungle Book* is more poignant than Mowgli's brief and ambivalent sojourn in the home of his presumed birth mother,

Kipling in his Naulakha study, with a statuette of Mowgli's wolf brother,
a gift of Joel Chandler Harris.

Messua, a kindly rural villager who doesn't know quite what to do—like many a mother since—when her teenage son wanders back into her life for a few weeks. It has become clear, to Mowgli and to us, that he will not be able to choose a mate from among the wolves or the monkeys. His only real future, even in a book as fantastical as this one, is with his own kind. Mowgli, who has grown up in the forest, is uncomfortable in his birth mother's hut, which feels like a trap to him; she is uncomfortable outside it, where wolves and tigers roam. One thing she does do, however, is give the child milk to drink, as though her nursing, interrupted so many years earlier, could now be resumed without complication. Suddenly, at this very moment, Mowgli feels something touch his foot. "Mother," says Mowgli, "what dost *thou* here?" It is Mother Wolf, his adoptive mother, licking his foot. "I have a desire to see that woman who gave thee milk," says Mother Wolf. Then she growls, possessively, "I gave thee thy first milk!"

Kipling often explored the imaginative possibilities of his stories by working out alternatives in his poems. In a poem written in Brattleboro around 1893, and included as an epigraph in early editions of *The Jungle Book*, he staged an encounter between a human birth mother and her wayward son, who is drawn to the night world of wolves. The poem is called "The Only Son," and its opening lines describe a mother's fear about noises in the night outside: "She dropped the bar, she shot the bolt, she fed the fire anew, / For she heard a whimper under the sill and a great grey paw came through."

Having secured the door, she does nothing more, but her son has an unsettling dream, related to that great gray paw: "Now was I born of womankind and laid in a mother's breast? / For I have dreamed of a shaggy hide whereon I went to rest." After a few more lines in this questioning vein, the Only Son asks his mother to unbar the door since, as he says, "I must out and see / If those are wolves that wait outside or my own kin to me!" The poem concludes as it began, from the mother's point of view: "She loosed the bar, she slid the bolt, she opened the door anon, / And a grey bitch-wolf came out of the dark and fawned on the Only Son!" Kipling has led us into another myth altogether, the familiar nightmare figure of the werewolf. The poem is a reminder of how original the treatment of Mowgli is by contrast, in which the wolves are a comforting, intimate family, a refuge from human turmoil and not, as in the poem, an intensification of it.

· 2 ·

Kipling's originality is even more striking when his account of Mowgli's adoption by wolves is contrasted with its Indian sources. He alludes to these accounts when Father Wolf tells Mother Wolf that he has heard of wolf adoptions, "but never in our Pack." Kipling's father had a particular interest in such stories. In his encyclopedic book *Beast and Man in India*, published in 1891, Lockwood Kipling wrote, "India is probably the cradle of wolf-child stories, which are here universally believed and supported by a cloud of testimony." One source that Kipling drew on for his Mowgli narrative is titled "An Account of Wolves Nurturing Children in Their Dens," written by W. H. Sleeman, a British official. Sleeman is best known today for his suppression of a secret criminal gang known as the Thuggee (from which the word "thug" is derived); Mark Twain was enchanted by Sleeman's account of his successful campaign. In 1849–50, however, Sleeman traveled throughout the Kingdom of Oude for the purpose of recommending measures to improve the region and the plight of its people. He was also supposed to provide evidence in support of the recent annexation of Oude by the British East India Company. During his travels, he claims to have heard many reports of wolves carrying off native children.

The six stories Sleeman reports have certain features in common. The children carried off by wolves are always native children, never British. They are always rescued by government officials, never by villagers. In those cases where parents recognize their children after their rescue, things do not go well; the parents give up the children for adoption or the children die. The behavior of the feral children, after their rescue from the dens of wolves, is remarkably similar in the six accounts. They have calluses on their elbows and knees from crawling around on all fours. They prefer raw to cooked meat. They tolerate the company of dogs when feeding. They are incapable of learning human language. They die young.

Sleeman appears to have thought that such consistency added to the credibility of the stories, but the repetitive details suggest instead their formulaic nature. All of the reports come from the same period, from about 1842 to 1848, with a cluster of three or four—Sleeman is not precise—dating from 1843, apparently a banner year for wolf adoptions. Such a concentration of stories in a particular place and time would suggest either an epidemic of wolf adoptions, as though the wolves had suddenly developed an appetite for raising human children rather than eating them, or a mass hysteria among villagers. Sleeman argues, however, that the Hindu villagers made a profit from their transactions with wolves, essentially trading their children for money. "It is remarkable that they very seldom catch Wolves, though they know all their dens, and could easily dig them out as they dig out other animals," he writes. "This is supposed to arise from the profit which they make by the gold and silver bracelets, necklaces, and other ornaments, which are worn by the children, whom the Wolves carry to their dens and devour, and are left at the entrance of these dens." He concludes with the damning observation, "In every part of India a great number of children are every day murdered for the sake of their ornaments."

One might think that this peculiar analysis would help explain why so many native children are *eaten* by wolves rather than *nurtured* by them. But for Sleeman, the devouring and the nurturing are part of the same pathology, namely that native Hindus, in his view, simply don't care very much for their children. The characterization of Indian peasantry that he is at pains to establish is that of careless and apathetic parents distracted by their work in the fields, as their children meanwhile are "carried off" by wolves. When the feral children are returned to them, the parents, appalled by their grunts and nasty smells, proceed to place the children, doubly lost to their parents, in charity care. The responsible parties in these stories are never the villagers, with their benighted family values, but rather the British officials and those employed by them. The need for European paternalism is triumphantly demonstrated at every turn. The local Hindus must be taught to value their children more than the gold bracelets on their wrists.

Kipling departed from these Indian sources in several key ways. He chose a native child for his hero, rather than a British official or child, and he portrayed Mowgli's native birth mother as a sympathetic figure. Kipling went further, in portraying the adoptive family of wolves with equal sympathy. One might compare, in this regard, the Mowgli stories with Edgar Rice Burroughs's eugenic fantasy *Tarzan of the Apes*, for which Burroughs borrowed many details from *The Jungle Book*, including a godlike hero of superhuman strength, agility, and physical beauty raised in the wild by ferocious animals. Burroughs departs from Kipling in his insistence that Tarzan's birth parents are English nobility, Lord and Lady Greystoke, and that what Tarzan learns about proper behavior does not come from the great apes who raise him but rather from the books his parents have left behind. Mowgli, by contrast, is adopted by friendly wolves that also happen to be model parents. He grows up not with calluses on his knees and elbows, cowering in the shadows like Sleeman's unfortunate waifs, but as an energetic and sensitive leader, powerful in mind and body, who can kill a tiger, make complicated moral choices, and right the wrongs in both human and animal communities.

3.

If Kipling relied in part on Indian sources for his tale of Mowgli among the wolves, he also drew on his Vermont surroundings, especially his conviction that he was living in a lawless jungle. "Kipling never quite outgrew his first impression that every American citizen carried concealed weapons of war," his friend Molly Cabot recalled. He had witnessed a murder in a San Francisco gambling den. He had watched an American woman enjoying the carnage of a Chicago slaughterhouse. Such experiences had left him convinced that violence was at the molten core of American life. As though to stave off the chaos that surrounded them, he and Carrie dressed each evening for dinner, much to the amusement of their more informal neighbors. Kipling considered himself, as a well-informed outsider, uniquely qualified to interpret this bloodthirsty society. He was "the only man living," he insisted to Cabot, "who could write The Great American Novel."

Kipling believed, furthermore, that America was "the place in which to create." His father summarized Rudyard's expansive view: "There is undoubtedly a freer outlook from America for the man who prefers to think for himself than from London." Kipling gleaned most of his useful information about his new surroundings from Cabot. Lively, sophisticated, and well read, she was a longtime friend of the Balestier family, long assumed to be Wolcott's future wife. She had never married, living alone in the handsome, upright house inherited from her father in the fashionable neighborhood of terraces near the Connecticut River, on the northern edge of Brattleboro. A dedicated antiquarian who wrote two volumes about her native city, Cabot was a steady fund of anecdotes and gossip for Kipling, as he eagerly sought out material for his own writing.

A passionate reader of American literature, high and low, Kipling was acutely aware of contemporary writing about ordinary lives lived in New England, the so-called "local color" school, which consisted primarily of women writers writing about women's subjects. Kipling was contemplating a volume of "Country Sketches," for which Cabot supplied photographs. These would be about women, since so many of the men had fled the farms and villages of Vermont for better prospects elsewhere. "It would be hard to exaggerate the loneliness and sterility of life on the farms," he wrote. "What might have become characters, powers, and attributes perverted themselves in that desolation as cankered trees throw out branches akimbo, and strange faiths and cruelties, born of solitude to the edge of insanity, flourished like lichen on sick bark." These were the resilient lives described by local-color masters like Mary Wilkins (later Freeman), who lived in Brattleboro, and Sarah Orne Jewett, based in Boston and Maine.

"It has been said that the New England stories are cramped and narrow," Kipling wrote in their staunch defense. "Even a far-off view of the iron-bound life whence they are drawn justifies the author. You can carve a nut in a thousand different ways by reason of the hardness of the shell."

Kipling's view might be called the netsuke theory of local-color writing: the harder the conditions, the more possibilities in describing them. One of the first guests the Kiplings welcomed to Bliss Cottage was Mary Wilkins. "I invite Miss Wilkins to come to us today for tiffin," Carrie wrote in her diary on October 11, 1892. With its spare furniture and bare floors, their tiny cottage could have been the setting for a typical Wilkins story of deprivation. Wilkins's sharp-edged stories about tough-minded women in villages and farms, such as "A New England Nun" and "A Poetess," appealed to Kipling, who once described a woman he had met in the neighboring village of Putney as "the best subject Mary Wilkins never wrote about."

And yet, perhaps out of respect for what writers like Wilkins and Jewett (whom he also befriended) had already accomplished, Kipling ultimately shied away from trying his hand at the dialect and the dilemmas of the local townsfolk. He wrote one fanciful story about personified locomotives in the Brattleboro railroad shed and another about loyal workhorses rejecting a new arrival who wants to organize them for a labor strike. Instead, he found his imagination fully engaged by a very different kind of local color—far beyond the villages, beyond the farms. "Beyond this desolation are woods where the bear and the deer still find peace," Kipling wrote, "and sometimes even the beaver forgets that he is persecuted and dares to build his lodge."

4.

Most persecuted of all the woodland animals, however, was the wolf. And it was the adventures of a family of wolves that began to take shape in Kipling's imagination amid the wolf-less hills of Vermont. Abundant timber, as Molly Cabot explained, had first attracted European adventurers and settlers to the banks of the Connecticut River: virgin forests and the abundant wild game that lived among them. Great logs of white pine, destined for ships in the British navy, were floated down the river from Vermont as early as 1733, and laws were soon established for licenses of exploitation, as well as for provisions regarding reforestation of the land.

The difficulties that these early lumbermen and their families encountered, as Molly Cabot noted, required "special energies of mind and body." She wrote of a Mrs. Dunklee, among the earliest settlers, who was chased by wolves while traveling on horseback, "and only escaped by climbing the branches of a tree, when the horse made his way home and brought the family to her rescue." Inspired in part by such horror stories of predatory wolves, vengeful hunters and trappers began targeting the wolves of New England. Wolves had not been welcome in the New England woods for a very long time, however. Among the first laws instituted by the Puritan settlers of the Massachusetts Bay Colony in 1630 was a bounty on wolves, which Roger Williams, who fled the colony for its religious intolerance, referred to as "a fierce, bloodsucking persecutor." Extermination of the New England wolf was complete two centuries later; according to the Massachusetts Division of Fisheries and Wildlife, the gray wolf has been extinct in the state since about 1840, fifty years before the Kiplings arrived in Vermont.

Brattleboro played an important part in the extermination of wolves. After the free-love activist John Humphrey Noyes was banished from Putney for transgressing local moral codes, he established the Oneida Community in upstate New York, hoping that agriculture would keep his followers alive. Animal traps designed by a Noyes adherent named Newhouse proved more lucrative. Oneida wolf traps soon dominated the market, as free love and wolf hatred proved compatible with sales pitches. The Newhouse trap, according to one advertisement, "going before the axe and the plow, forms the prow with which iron-clad civilization is pushing back barbaric solitude, causing the bear and beaver to give way to the wheat field, the library and the piano." Oneida traps were widely used in New England and the West, where strychnine inserted into buffalo corpses helped wipe out the wolf population.

At precisely the moment that wolves disappeared from New England, some prominent New Englanders began to miss them. By the mid-nineteenth century, New England sages were already lamenting the loss of wildness in both landscape and society. They invoked wolves rather than bald eagles as a sort of national icon. In the epigraph to his classic essay "Self-Reliance," Ralph Waldo Emerson admonished his countrymen to embrace a regime of tough love—to cast their "bantlings," their young children, into the wilderness and have them learn to fend for themselves.

> Cast the bantling on the rocks,
> Suckle him with the she-wolf's teat;
> Wintered with the hawk and fox,
> Power and speed be hands and feet.

Henry David Thoreau expanded the allure of a Romulus-and-Remus education in the wild: "It is because the children of the empire were not suckled by wolves that they were conquered & displaced by the children of the northern forests who were." Throwing down the national gauntlet, Thoreau added, "America is the she wolf today."

Emerson was a particular favorite of Kipling. He felt that his adopted home in Brattleboro was underwritten by Emerson, since the Sage of Concord had written admiringly of Mount Monadnock in his poetic series "Woodnotes." Monadnock happened to have its own conspicuous place in New England legends about wolves. The woods around the mountain had been repeatedly clear-cut and burned to prevent wolves from taking refuge in the supposed wolf pits among the rocky outcroppings. The mountain's bare face was thus a monument to wolf hatred. Emerson's "Self-Reliance" was more than a favorite essay for Kipling; it was a sacred creed to live by. Kipling's poem "If—" is a recasting of Emerson's idea of self-trust. "If you can trust yourself when all men doubt you, / But make allowance for their doubting too; / . . . You'll be a Man, my son!" Kipling writes. Kipling's choice of wolves for Mowgli's ideal family may well have been inspired, in part, by the epigraph from "Self-Reliance": "Suckle him with the she-wolf's teat."

The belief that there were benefits of an education in the wild was widespread by the 1890s, when there was pervasive fear in the United States that the country was becoming overcivilized, a land of sissies unprepared for the onslaught of the immigrant hordes flooding the country. Wolves, however, were not always considered a part of this idealized life in the wild. Theodore Roosevelt drew a distinction between noble wild beasts worthy of preservation—such as deer, moose, and bears—and ignoble beasts. The wolf, in Roosevelt's view, was "the beast of waste and desolation." Bears should be hunted; wolves should be exterminated.

5.

Kipling's vivid narrative in the Mowgli chapters of *The Jungle Book* is less driven by tooth and claw—the naturalist vision of Roosevelt and Jack London—than by a psychological conflict. The abandoned man-cub Mowgli is torn between his wild identity as a brother of the wolves who take him in and his dawning sense, as he is taught by Bagheera, the black panther born in captivity, that he rightly belongs among men. "I am two Mowglis," he laments. "These two things fight together in me as snakes fight in the spring." For Bagheera, however, this anguished status of being in between is actually a source of strength. "Yes, I too was born among men," Bagheera tells Mowgli, recounting his years in the private zoo of an Indian king and showing the mark of the collar on his neck, "and because I had learned the ways of men, I became more terrible in the jungle than Shere Khan." The question for Mowgli—as it so often is for Kipling—is to find the proper balance between the claims of civilization and the claims of the wild.

In 1907, Sigmund Freud answered a request from a publisher for a list of ten good books. The books on Freud's list were, as he put it, "'good' friends, to whom one owes a portion of one's knowledge of life and one's world view." The second entry on Freud's list was *The Jungle Book*, a great favorite of his. One can easily see why the story of a child raised by wolves appealed to Freud, who had reimagined childhood—that innocent realm of the buttoned-up Victorians—as a battleground of contending forces: sexual, aggressive, and wild. Civilization, in Freud's view, was built on the repression of these forces, but at a considerable cost to human satisfaction. "Kipling's lesson seems plain," writes Peter Gay, Freud's biographer. "Men cover up their libido and their aggressiveness behind bland and mendacious surfaces; animals are superior beings, for they acknowledge their drives." One can see why Max, that latter-day Mowgli, wears his wolf suit when he goes on his night journey in *Where the Wild Things Are*. And one can see why *The Jungle Book*, that vivid story of adoption by wolves, was as close as Kipling came, after all his conversations with Mary Cabot, to writing the Great American Novel.

their isolated Vermont farm, buried in snow and exposed to every kind of weather New England could inflict.

Kipling had his own reasons to get away. He craved a fresh direction for his writing, as he continued to add exotic tales to his *Jungle Book*. Travel and inspiration had always been closely associated in his mind. A first stab at the narrative that would eventually grow into *Kim* had persuaded him that a visit to northern India might help him more fully to imagine the setting and the characters. He envisaged something like his journey across the United States in 1889, with letters sent home (in this case to New York) for publication. In the meantime, there was the prospect of Washington. He confided to the Harvard art historian Charles Eliot Norton (a friend of his father who had traveled in India during his youth) on the eve of departure: "I have a yearning upon me to tell tales of extended impropriety—not sexual or within hailing distance of it—but hard-bottomed unseemly yarns." He added, "One can't be serious always."

After finding their first rooms in Washington intolerable, the Kiplings checked into the newly opened Grafton Hotel on fashionable Connecticut Avenue, expensive and not very comfortable, in Carrie's snobbish opinion. But there was good company to be had nearby. Henry Adams was traveling in the Caribbean, but Adams's close friend John Hay was in town. A novelist, dialect poet, Anglophile, and future secretary of state in the William McKinley administration, Hay had also served, as a young man, as Lincoln's private secretary. Adams and Hay cultivated a group of promising younger men. Kipling had already met one of them, Cecil Spring Rice, a member of the British legation, in Tokyo. Hay and Spring Rice, accompanied by their wives, were the Kiplings' first visitors at the Grafton Hotel. Another rising young man in the circle was twenty-six-year-old Theodore Roosevelt, a civil service commissioner. "I liked him from the first," Kipling wrote of Roosevelt. Rounding off the group was William Hallett Phillips, a Washington lawyer, congressional insider, and expert on American Indians, destined to be Kipling's closest friend in what Adams called the "little Washington gang."

Had Kipling been more attentive, he could have heard "tales of extended impropriety" among his new Washington friends. For what he had stumbled upon, among the elms and gardens around Lafayette Square, was, in effect, an American Bloomsbury. John Hay had a romantic understanding with Nellie Lodge, wife of Henry Cabot Lodge, the powerful Massachusetts senator. Henry Adams, bereft after the suicide of his wife, Clover, was passionately in love with Elizabeth Cameron, wife of a dissipated senator from Pennsylvania. Hay was also secretly courting Lizzie Cameron, while trying not to step on his best friend's toes. Yet another intimate of this circle was the prominent geologist Clarence King, who had secretly married an African-American woman in New York, in whose company he managed to "pass" as a black Pullman porter.

2.

A popular destination for these leisured aristocrats was the National Zoological Park, established by Congress in 1889 and first opened to the public in 1891. The National Zoo was placed under the administrative auspices of Samuel Langley, director of the Smithsonian Institution. The original conception was double: to amuse and instruct the urban inhabitants while preserving native species threatened by overhunting and the timber industry. The grounds were laid out by Frederick Law Olmsted, the designer of New York's Central Park, on 166 forested acres along Rock Creek in northwest Washington. Here, Kipling and his new friends could talk freely, safely out of public view.

The zoo's first director was William Temple Hornaday, a taxidermist by trade and a fierce advocate of wildlife preservation. Hornaday had assembled a Noah's Ark of 185 animals, sheltered in makeshift pens and cages on the Washington Mall, adjoining the Smithsonian's main building. Hornaday's menagerie, which he originally used as his taxidermy models, became the first inhabitants of the zoo. These included, according to Smithsonian records, "buffalo, a black bear, woodchucks, a panther, a grizzly bear cub, a Carolina black bear, a bald eagle, turkey vultures, and black snakes."

The charms of the zoo were not lost on Kipling. He was adding stories to *The Jungle Book*, and the animals he encountered at the zoo confirmed details in the narrative. The zoo also brought him fresh ideas for further stories. Spring Rice, Phillips, and Roosevelt escorted Kipling to the Smithsonian, where Langley gave him various publications, including one on Inuit culture. One such pamphlet inspired the story "Quiquern," in *The Second Jungle Book*, about two sled dogs. The young men then proceeded to the zoo, where Kipling, according to Spring Rice, "was like a child and roared with laughter at the elephants and the bears." More pilgrimages followed, and the zoo soon became Kipling's favorite Washington destination. Roosevelt made it clear that he wanted to show off the bears to his new friend. As Kipling recalled in *Something of Myself,* he and Roosevelt "would go off to the Zoo together," where Roosevelt "talked about grizzlies that he had met"—presumably on his hunting forays in the Rockies.

3.

One particular grizzly bear on display in the National Zoo that winter had a special meaning for Kipling's Washington circle. This group of men—rich, well educated, and socially connected—shared a passion for hunting, in a style that they associated with the European-landed aristocracy. Hallett Phillips and Theodore Roosevelt were founding members of the Boone and Crockett Club, named for a couple of national heroes known for their prowess with a rifle. Established in 1887, the club was a coterie of wealthy big-game hunters who adopted an aristocratic code, known as the "Fair Chase Statement," for the proper "taking" of animals, without recourse to traps, nets, and the like. Members were to engage in a "one-to-one relationship with the quarry" and pledged to take their prey "in a manner that does not give the hunter an improper advantage." The club lobbied Congress to protect wilderness spaces and had won an early victory when it rallied support for the expansion of Yellowstone, the nation's first national park. Members also took an interest in the building of zoos, essentially game preserves by a different name.

The greatest achievement of the Boone and Crockett Club was the federal legislation that established the national forests. Hunters like Phillips and Roosevelt had long worried that rapacious timber companies were destroying the natural habitat of big game—the bison, elk, and grizzly bears that they loved to hunt. According to Roosevelt, the average westerner had "but one thought about a tree, and that was to cut it down." In 1891, Phillips slipped a provision into a congressional spending bill calling for the "reserving" of public lands. What came to be known as the Forest Reserve Act passed on March 3. According to the historian Charles Beard, the act was "one of the most noteworthy measures ever passed in the history of the nation."

In recognition of this legislative victory, Adams invited a group of close friends, including Hay and Phillips, on a hunting and fishing trip to Yellowstone during the summer of 1894. They met in Chicago, crippled at the time by the great Pullman Strike. "The strike can hardly affect us much," Adams assured Hay on July 13, a couple of days after US marshals had arrested Eugene Debs and suppressed the strike by force. Adams, whose brother Charles Francis Adams was president of the Union Pacific Railroad, could count on John Hay to share his negative assessment of the strikers. Hay had married the daughter of a Cleveland steel baron; in his bestselling novel *The Bread-winners* (1883), the villain is a labor organizer. By the end of July, the hunting party had reached their hotel in Yellowstone. Adams, who had accompanied his friend Clarence King on his forays for the US Geological Survey, claimed that there wasn't much left to hunt. "Compared with the Rockies of 1871, the sense of wildness had vanished," he complained. "Only the more intelligent ponies scented an occasional friendly and sociable bear."

One such bear was destined for the National Zoo. Henry Adams playfully wrote to Martha Cameron, the young daughter of Elizabeth Cameron, reporting that news had reached their hotel that "a man had caught a big grizzly bear about seven miles above us," adding, "Perhaps Mr. Langley will take him to the zoo, and you may see him there." By October, the grizzly from Yellowstone was safely ensconced in Langley's zoo. "Tell Martha that Bill Flips [William Phillips] and I went out to the Zoo last Sunday to see her bear," Adams informed Lizzie Cameron. "It is so wild that it has to be put in a house by itself, where it was sore trying to break the bars." Evidently, this Yellowstone specimen was one of the bears—"rather too big to lead home with a string," Adams joked—that Roosevelt wanted Kipling to admire at the Washington Zoo.

4.

Kipling enjoyed Teddy Roosevelt's boisterous company. And yet the two new friends differed on key points. They quarreled at the Smithsonian over the status of American Indians, whom Kipling had always admired for their self-reliance in the wilderness. "I never got over the wonder," Kipling wrote in *Something of Myself*, "of a people who, having extirpated the aboriginals of their continent more completely than any modern race had ever done, honestly believed that they were a godly little New England community, setting examples to brutal mankind." He shared his amazement with Roosevelt, "who made the glass cases of Indian relics shake with his rebuttals." It also became clear that Kipling wasn't particularly interested in Roosevelt's bears. He was far more interested in the *beavers*.

During his 1889 journey across the American continent, Kipling had spent a few days in Yellowstone. On a trail ride along the Firehole River, he had sought out a beaver lodge. "The question was, would they come out for their walk before it got too dark to see." The question was soon answered. "They came—blessings on their blunt muzzles, they came—as shadows come, drifting down the stream, stirring neither foot nor tail," he wrote. "There were three of them. One went down to investigate the state of the dam; the other two began to look for supper. There is only one thing more startling than the noiselessness of a tiger in the jungle, and that is the noiselessness of a beaver in the water." Kipling looked at the beavers at work with an almost religious awe. Having "seen the beaver in his wilds," Kipling vowed, "never will I go to the Zoo."

Five years later, Kipling was not only going to the zoo; he was going there repeatedly. Studying the beaver colony became a major preoccupation during his final days in Washington. Carrie's diary for March 29 has a single entry: "R visiting the beavers at the zoo." The beavers worked tirelessly—worked, as Kipling noted, "with the cold-chisel," building dams, dens, and lakes.

What Kipling admired in his beloved beavers was a colonial world in miniature. What Roosevelt admired in bears, by contrast, was their brute marauding strength. One might discern in the two friends' diverging views two contrasting notions of empire. For Kipling, empire was a realm of responsibilities. For Roosevelt, empire was a world of opportunities. The primary aim of empire, for TR, was territorial expansion through glorious war. It is tempting to believe that these opposing views of empire—as public service and as territorial conquest—were partially established while Kipling and Roosevelt, those two celebrants of empire, strolled through the Washington Zoo, talking and arguing, during the spring of 1895.

5.

Carrie and Rudyard returned to Brattleboro on April 6, their journey delayed by torrential rains, and found a world underwater. One of the annual spring "freshets," fueled by melting snow and the contours of the Vermont landscape, had submerged Brattleboro and their own access road in one of the worst floods of the city's history. By mid-April, with the waters receding, Kipling reported to a friend that watching the beavers had been the high point of the Washington trip. "When the head of the Washington Zoo let me frolic in private enclosures where the beaver lived, and postponed feeding the beasts till I found it convenient to come, I felt that Notoriety was beginning to be worth something." For Kipling had a dream as he eyed the swollen brooks and the incessant rain. His dream was to reintroduce the beaver to the wetlands of Vermont, where they had died out by the 1850s, victims of deforestation and the fur trade.

A month later, he was still full of excitement about his "experiences with beaver" in Washington. He wrote to the New York publisher Ripley Hitchcock, an amateur naturalist: "How I met Bill Hofer the trapper who trapped 'em; how I was introduced to the whole seven of 'em that made the dam in the Zoo (such a Zoo!); how I got photographs of the said dam in three lights and finally how I went into the fencing question with the head of the Zoo." The fencing question turned out to be the rub. Kipling wanted an enclosure for his Vermont beavers, to keep the beavers in a little private zoo of his own rather than allow them to increase and multiply—into the garden that he and Carrie had been building, and up and down the banks of the Connecticut River. "It's beyond my means because *unless* you sink sheet iron or concrete five feet below ground the beaver will burrow out," he concluded. "Everything else would be as easy as falling off a log but I can't fence ten acres in that way."

6.

Another of Kipling's dreams that summer had a better result. Tired of riding, or sledding, into Brattleboro to get his voluminous mail—often as many as two hundred letters a day—he had hit on an alternative: a post office of his own, down where the road to his house intersected with Putney Road. He asked his new friend William Hallett Phillips to approach the McKinley administration with the request. In mid-June, Kipling was gratified to learn that the petition had been approved. "After this," he wrote Phillips, in the mock-Indian banter that had become habitual with them, "the name of Sitting Fox [his nickname for Phillips] shall be entered among the Trues [the Indian gods]. His Lodge shall be in the center of the camp, painted and crowned with feathers."

Kipling invited Phillips to visit Naulakha. Phillips combined many qualities that Kipling admired: he was bookish, informal, generous, adventurous, and loved the outdoors. He was also of good (and colorful) family. Kipling had a weakness for Southerners and the Lost Cause. Phillips's father, Philip, had represented Alabama in Congress until the firing on Fort Sumter, when the family—with the help of Philip's friend Edwin Stanton, later Lincoln's secretary of war—was allowed to return to the South, but not before his wife, Eugenia Levy Phillips, from one of Charleston's prominent Jewish families, was arrested for suspicion of promoting Confederate interests. Kipling told Phillips that he had a job for him "*much* more important than PO's," namely, to build "a wigwam, wickyup, whaire or whatever its name is" for Josephine.

Phillips arrived in Brattleboro in early September, on his way back to Washington from John Hay's estate in New Hampshire. Kipling and Phillips spent long hours in the woods, or the "jungle" as Kipling called it, telling each other Indian legends, both authentic (Phillips) and invented (Kipling). Each morning, Phillips would "hear Kipling's voice challenging me to go forth" into the jungle, he reported to Hay. "Into it

Josephine on the porch of Naulakha, with a tiger skin for a blanket.

we crawl, and I listen to what the Master of the Jungle tells; and what talk!... What a wonder that fellow is! What felicity and what fecundity." A few years later, the escapades provided material for Kipling's *Just So Stories*, with Josephine dressed as Pocahontas, and father and daughter honoring their totem animal, the beaver.

7.

Two selections from Kipling's *Just So Stories*, "How the First Letter Was Written" and "How the Alphabet Was Made," evoke the September idyll when Bill Phillips came to Naulakha to build a wigwam and to receive thanks for the post office. On the face of it, they tell the whimsical story of the invention of writing by a "Neolithic man" and his clever daughter, and how they sent the first letter through the mail. In "How the First Letter Was Written," Tegumai and his daughter, Taffy, venture out from their cave by the beaver swamp to go fishing in the Wagai River. Trying to stab a carp, Tegumai breaks his spear, and Taffy hits on an ingenious way to alert her mother, Teshumai Tewindrow. "I say, Daddy, it's an awful nuisance that you and I don't know how to write, isn't it?" she says brightly. "If we did we could send a message for the new spear." A "Stranger-man" turns up and hands Taffy a "big flat piece of bark off a birch-tree" meant to show "that his heart was as white as the birch-bark." Taffy sees the birch bark differently. "You want my Mummy's living address?" she asks. "Of course I can't write, but I can draw pictures if I've anything sharp to scratch with. Please lend me the shark's tooth off your necklace."

And Taffy draws a picture of Tegumai's plight, broken spear and all. This is the first letter, and Taffy, "drawing very hard and rather scratchily," provides the address as well, replete with beavers. Taffy's drawing is open to multiple interpretations. The Stranger reads it as Tegumai's plea for help against his enemies "coming up on all sides with spears." Teshumai Tewindrow assumes instead that the Stranger himself has stuck the spear into Tegumai, "'and here are a whole pack of people' (they were Taffy's beavers really, but they did look rather like people) 'coming up behind Tegumai.'" Everything is soon sorted out, and Taffy is assured that she has "hit upon a great invention," and that (punning on the two meanings of "letters") "a time will come, O Babe of Tegumai, when we shall make letters—all twenty-six of 'em—and when we shall be able to read as well as to write, and then we shall always say exactly what we mean without any mistakes."

And that is exactly what happens in "How the Alphabet Was Made," as father and daughter invent twenty-six different "noise-pictures," one for each letter of the alphabet. Many of the letters scratched on birch bark are derived from animals: *A* is the sound a carp might make, gasping for air. *B* is for "beaver," the sacred totem of Tegumai's tribe. Kipling's illustration shows its evolution from pictograph to stylized *B*. As Taffy invents one letter after another, her father realizes how momentous their invention is. It is, he tells her, "*the* big secret of the world." Tegumai is so excited that he makes "a magic Alphabet-necklace of all the letters, so that it could be put in the Temple of Tegumai and kept forever and ever."

8.

Another celebration of Bill Phillips's visit was a spring poem that Kipling wrote in March 1897. "The Feet of the Young Men" is a love poem, really, and recalls "The Long Trail" in its yearning call to fellow vagabonds to join the poet on the open road.

> Now the Four-way Lodge is opened, now the Hunting
>   Winds are loose—
> Now the Smokes of Spring go up to clear the brain;
> Now the Young Men's hearts are troubled for the whisper
>   of the Trues,
> Now the Red Gods make their medicine again!
> Who hath seen the beaver busied? Who hath watched the
>   black-tail mating?
> Who hath lain alone to hear the wild-goose cry?

The idyllic destination is the all-male precincts of the camp. "Let him follow with the others, for the Young Men's feet are turning / To the camps of proved desire and known delight!" There, a man, "waiting as a lover," might indulge in a "misty sweat-bath": "And to each a man that knows his naked soul!" The poem, which owes something to Baude-laire's "L'invitation au voyage," later became a favorite of the Boy Scouts.

Kipling was about to mail the poem to Phillips when he received the terrible news that his friend, on just such a camping trip as he had imag-ined, had accidentally drowned in the Potomac River. "I had just written out in full *his* special copy of the 'Red Gods' and was getting ready to mail it," Kipling wrote that May. "Now all I can do is to dedicate the thing to his memory." Kipling must have noted the eerie parallel with "The Long Trail," which had been written to another intimate male friend, Wolcott Balestier, just before *his* death in Dresden.

The Boone and Crockett Club held its annual meeting the following January at the Metropolitan Club in New York. Teddy Roosevelt, who had risen to the rank of assistant secretary of the navy, took the train up from Washington. There was much to celebrate, notably the establish-ment of the Bronx Zoo, another urban game preserve that the club had vigorously supported. But there was also the sad news about Phillips, a founding member of the club. "Among the toasts . . . will be a silent one to the memory of William Hallett Phillips of Washington, who was ac-cidentally drowned in the Potomac River last spring." Phillips, *The New York Times* noted, "was numbered among the few very intimate friends of Rudyard Kipling, and to his memory Kipling dedicated his last stirring poem in *Scribner's Magazine* entitled 'The Feet of the Young Men.'"

9.

Five years later, in 1902, Theodore Roosevelt was in his first full year as president of the United States, after an assassin's bullet killed William McKinley. During his many years of hunting, Roosevelt had bagged many different kinds of big game, many bears in particular, but never a Louisiana black bear. When the governor of Mississippi suggested a bear hunt in the Delta swamp led by the legendary guide Holt Collier, Roosevelt eagerly accepted. Collier, a former slave and scout of the Confederate army, was known to have killed more than three thousand bears.

Collier knew the whereabouts of one mature bear in particular, and he had a plan. He placed Roosevelt in a blind, and instructed him to wait for a clear shot. Then he led his forty dogs into the dense tangle of virgin oak and cypress, with knee-high briars to plow through. It took several hours to bring the bear to bay, at which point Collier drove the bear, in a dangerous and delicate operation, toward the president's blind. But the president wasn't there. Impatient and hungry, he had taken a break for lunch. Collier, disgusted—"I could have killed him a thousand times," he said of the bear—then adopted plan B, even more dangerous. With the dogs harassing the bear, he managed to club it, lasso it, and drag it, slightly dazed, to a willow tree, where he tied it. Then he went in search of the president and invited him to shoot his bear.

Roosevelt was in awe of what Collier had done but refused to shoot a bear tied to a tree. It went against everything that the Boone and Crockett Club stood for. The "Fair Chase Statement" required the hunter to take his prey "in a manner that does not give the hunter an improper advantage." A bear tied to a tree surely offered the hunter an improper advantage. Collier's feat was widely celebrated in the national press, but it was Roosevelt's refusal—and his preference for lunch over hunting—that had the greater notoriety. Clifford Berryman drew a cartoon in *The Washington Post* of reluctant Roosevelt, his Rough Rider hat on his head and his rifle butt on the ground, with the caption "Drawing the Line in Mississippi." Instead of an old bear, Berryman drew a cute little black bear with ears that look fit for a mouse.

The little bear cub lived on. Morris Michtom, a shopkeeper in Brooklyn, made stuffed animals for toys. He designed a toy bear based on Berryman's drawing and called it "Teddy's Bear," securing the president's permission to market it, at a $1.50 per bear. So successful was his teddy bear that Michtom founded the Ideal Toy Corporation in 1903. By

Clifford Berryman, Drawing the Line in Mississippi.

1938, when Michtom died, Ideal Toy was selling more than a hundred thousand teddy bears a year. It seems a missed opportunity, in retrospect, that Michtom did not also make a stuffed animal called Ruddy Beaver, with Kipling's familiar round-lensed glasses, his unmistakable shaggy eyebrows, and his rounded head.

Chapter Nine

_____

A FISHING TRIP

I.

President Grover Cleveland loved to go fishing. Not fly-fishing, which he considered a deplorable affectation of pretentious purists, but plain old fishing, with a bobber, a sinker, and a baited hook. During the summer, the president fished every day at his retreat on Cape Cod. In the fall, he fished on the Potomac or on the Outer Banks in North Carolina. He fished "through hunger and heat, lightning and tempest," wrote Richard Watson Gilder, editor of *Century Magazine* and a frequent companion on the president's leisurely outings. A large and slow-moving man, Cleveland weighed 240 pounds and disliked exercise. "Bodily movement alone," he wrote, "is among the dreary and unsatisfying things of life." But the president liked to fish and he liked to hunt— preferably sitting down, in a blind, from dawn to dark. When the cares of office weighed on him, he grabbed a fishing rod or a gun and lit out for the territory. The president "was immoderate in only two things," Gilder wrote, "his deskwork and his fishing."

What drove Cleveland to the North Carolina coast, during the late fall of 1895, was a hostile note from the British prime minister, Lord Salisbury. British Guiana, colonized during the early nineteenth century, shared a border with Venezuela, though the precise location of the boundary had long been in question. When gold was discovered in the disputed region, the British reasserted their claim to the Orinoco River, deep in Venezuela territory. Venezuela appealed to the United States to serve as a neutral arbitrator between the rival claimants. Cleveland accepted, prompting outrage from Lord Salisbury.

It was not the first time that the president had tangled with Great Britain over boundaries and natural resources. During his first term, there were testy negotiations over fishing rights in the North Atlantic. There was also a boundary dispute between Alaska and British Columbia—where gold was again at issue—and a debate about the declining population of fur seals in the Bering Sea, which inspired Kipling's story "The White Seal." (Included in *The Jungle Book*, the story is about a seal who leads thousands of his comrades to safety, away from the depredations of merciless hunters armed with clubs.) But the Venezuelan crisis was different, and the stakes were higher. American interests were not involved, as the British pointed out, so what should a president do? The US Navy was negligible; Britannia, by contrast, ruled the waves. The president, as was his habit at such times, packed his guns and headed south to think about his response.

The duck hunting was excellent. The president returned pumped up and resolved. He consulted with his bellicose secretary of state, Richard Olney, and stayed up all night writing a response to the British ultimatum. "I am ... firm in my conviction," he wrote, "that, while it is a grievous thing to contemplate the two great English-speaking peoples of the world as being otherwise than friendly competitors in the onward march of civilization and strenuous and worthy rivals in all the arts of peace, there is no calamity which a great nation can invite which equals that which follows a supine submission to wrong and injustice and the consequent loss of national self-respect and honor, beneath which are shielded and defended a people's safety and greatness."

President Cleveland's "twenty-inch gun" message was widely interpreted as a threat of war. What the president had done was to invoke, for the first time, the Monroe Doctrine—the view that in American affairs, the interests of the United States took priority over European concerns—as the basis of American foreign policy in the western hemisphere. Support for Cleveland's belligerent stance was widespread in both political parties. Henry Cabot Lodge, the Massachusetts senator who dreamed of an American empire to rival Britain and Spain, led the call for war, along with his protégé, Theodore Roosevelt, who wildly imagined that the United States might lay claim to Canada as well. "This country needs a war," Roosevelt wrote to Lodge in December 1895, and ascribed opposition to "a flabby, timid type of character which eats away at the great fighting qualities of our race."

2.

Kipling was appalled by all the saber rattling. He felt betrayed by his friends in Washington, betrayed by his neighbors in Vermont, betrayed by his adopted country. "This folly puts an end to my good and wholesome life here," he wrote on January 8, 1896. The Venezuela dispute struck him as personally insulting, as if, he told Charles Eliot Norton, he had been "aimed at with a decanter across a friendly dinner table." Kipling had never liked President Cleveland. When John Hay had invited him, during his Washington visit, to meet the president and his cabinet, Kipling had found them "a colossal agglomeration of reeking bounders—awful; inexpressible; incredible." This surprising response to the dignified and honest president—"the sole reasonable facsimile of a major President between Lincoln and Theodore Roosevelt," in the view of historian Richard Hofstadter—owed something to the social disdain that Henry Adams and his circle—fly fishermen all—had for Cleveland. And besides, Kipling's dear friend Wolcott Balestier had written a campaign biography for Cleveland's opponent, James Blaine.

As threats of war escalated, Kipling had wild thoughts of escaping over the border into Canada. He met with a lawyer to ensure that Carrie, pregnant with their second child, was provided for if he were to join the British navy. "If the American mine is sprung," he wrote to Norton two weeks later, "it means dirt and slush and ultimately death [for me] either across the Canada border or in some disemboweled gunboat off Cape Hatteras." Kipling had a great deal on his mind and so—just like the overworked president—he packed his rods and went fishing. His companion was James Conland, the family doctor, who presided over the birth of the Kiplings' second daughter, Elsie, on February 2.

Kipling was particularly curious about Conland's experiences as a teenager, thirty years earlier, in the fishing fleets of Gloucester, Massachusetts. An idea was taking shape in his imagination for a quintessentially American story, about the heroic old days of the New England mariner. He wanted to capture, as he wrote in *Something of Myself,* "a rather beautiful localized American atmosphere that was already beginning to fade." The novel would also expose the current brash, bullying, moneygrubbing America that had stumbled into the Venezuelan crisis. He thought of calling the story, after its young hero, "Harvey Cheyne: Banker," with a pun on fishermen of the Grand Banks ("bankers") and the rich Cheyne family with its millions in the bank. Kipling titled the book *Captains Courageous* instead, borrowing a phrase from an old ballad of life at sea.

Captains Courageous was to be a fishing trip of the imagination, something to take Kipling's mind off the Anglo-American crisis. Always obsessed with getting the details right, Kipling made sure that some real fishing, off the coast of Boston and the North Shore town of Gloucester, got mixed in. On one such trip, Dr. Conland showed him, with a surgeon's skill, how cod was cut up and stowed in salt and ice, and got him aboard a fishing boat in Boston Harbor. Deeply seasick, Kipling watched the men hauling pollock from the surging sea before he fainted, only to be brought to his senses by the pungent smell of rotting fish, the smelling salts of the North Atlantic.

3.

Captains Courageous came quickly. As Carrie tended to the newborn baby down the hall, he had the whole story on paper within a month. He wrote proudly to his friend Robert Barr: "I'm most through with my first genuine out and out American story—a long one—. . . and oh Robert it is a beauty." He summarized the plot of this "boy's story" to the American writer Elizabeth Stuart Phelps Ward:

> The son of a western millionaire going to Europe with his mother, badly spoiled, falls overboard from a liner and is picked up by a dory of a Gloucester schooner. He is carried to the boat and his statements about his father's wealth and his own pocket-money are set down to the ravings of insanity. The schooner can't leave the banks in May, and so he is set to work as a second boy and goes through all the Bank experiences from trawling to witnessing a collision, and the gathering of the fleet round the Virgin. The three months experience makes a man of him or rather—he is only 15 years old—teaches him how to appreciate his father.

The book had "no plot; no love making and no social problem," Kipling insisted. "The boy works out his own salvation and learns discipline and duty."

As Kipling saw it, wealthy Americans were bored in their steam-powered conveyances on the land and sea. They could travel faster, like young Harvey Cheyne on his luxury liner bound for his expensive schooling in Europe, but they had no meaningful destination. Their amusements were for distraction only, their cultivation of the habits of maturity as empty as extinguished cigars. The first sentence of the novel strikes the note of the air-conditioned nightmare: "The weather door of the smoking-room had been left open to the North Atlantic fog, as the big liner rolled and lifted, whistling to warn the fishing-fleet." Harvey Cheyne begs a cigar and wonders aloud, with the sadistic boredom of privileged youth, what might lift the tedium. "Say, it's thick outside. You can hear the fish-boats squawking all around us. Say, wouldn't it be great if we ran down one?"

Sickened by the unfamiliar cigar, Harvey ventures onto the deserted deck and collapses against the guardrail. "Then a low, gray mother-wave swung out of the fog, tucked Harvey under one arm, so to speak, and pulled him off and away to leeward; the great green closed over him, and he went quietly to sleep." Instead of running down a fishing boat, Harvey Cheyne is rescued by one. "I make a big fish of you," says the kindly Portuguese fisherman, Manuel, who scoops him up from the waves like a squirming cod. With its rescued waif raised to responsible manhood, Kipling's narrative recalls Mowgli's toughening up in his adoptive family of wolves, with the "gray mother-wave" replacing Mowgli's gray Mother Wolf and the skilled fishermen standing in for Baloo and Bagheera.

Harvey's ensuing shipboard education goes beyond the learning of a manual (hence "Manuel") trade. His lessons are both spiritual and aesthetic, a deep gauging of his place in the natural scheme of things. The skipper Disko steers the *We're Here* through thick fog to "the edge of the barren Whale-deep, the blank hole of the Grand Bank." The narrative turns gothic: "A whiteness moved in the whiteness of the fog with a breath like the breath of the grave, and there was a roaring, a plunging, and spouting." Kipling's wording, here and elsewhere, recalls *Moby-Dick*, and specifically Melville's great chapter "The Whiteness of the Whale."

Kipling wrote with relish of the rules and rituals on a fishing vessel, and some of his most imaginative writing conveys the ways in which these skilled fishermen pursued their quarry. "When Disko thought of cod he thought as a cod; and by some long-tested mixture of instinct and experience, moved the *We're Here* from berth to berth, always with the fish, as a blindfolded chess-player moves on the unseen board." Kipling isn't quite finished with this ghostly metaphor. "But Disko's board was the grand Bank—a triangle two hundred and fifty miles on each side— a waste of wallowing sea, cloaked with dank fog, vexed with gales, harried with drifting ice, scored by the tracks of the reckless liners, and dotted with the sails of the fishing-fleet."

4.

It has been said that Harvey's conversion from spoiled brat to skilled fisherman happens too fast. But when Kipling assured Elizabeth Ward that there was no plot in *Captains Courageous*, he wasn't conceding a weakness in the book. He was signaling its true nature, as a sequence of picaresque episodes transmuted into visual scenes. The narrative is deliberately impressionistic—"I tried to get it thin, and tinny, and without passion," Kipling told Charles Eliot Norton, his art historian friend. It is a *painterly* book, and its closest analogy is not with the sentimental stories of Gloucester fisherfolk by Ward and others, but rather with the paintings of Winslow Homer, who depicted Gloucester and the Grand Banks in a trio of linked masterpieces. These three paintings—*The Herring Net, The Fog Warning*, and *Lost on the Grand Banks*—are the best guide to *Captains Courageous*. They comprise a powerful narrative sequence, as was immediately recognized when they were first exhibited together in 1885, and again, with even more éclat, at the World's Fair in Chicago in 1893.

Winslow Homer, The Fog Warning *(Museum of Fine Arts, Boston).*

Fog is a clear and present danger in all three paintings, as it is in Kipling's novel. The fishermen in their wave-tossed dories are separated by fogbanks from the safety of the "mother-ship." But fog is also, for Homer, an invitation for loose, freehanded brushwork, invading—almost enshrouding—the monumental figures of the men going about their tasks: lifting herring from the laden nets, with the schooner visible on the distant horizon in the first painting; rowing desperately, huge halibut in tow, for the mother ship about to be engulfed by an ominous fogbank in the second; and, in the third painting, looking over the brow of the boat for any sign of the mother ship in the surrounding dark fog.

Captains Courageous evoked themes ubiquitous in American novels of the time. Mired in a deep economic depression, the country cast about for where things had gone wrong. There was a prevalent sense that the rising generation was "soft," unworthy of the battle-tested heroic generation that had fought the Civil War. Teddy Roosevelt and his friends Owen Wister and Frederic Remington looked to the West for the "strenuous life" that might harden Americans for an uncharted future. Meanwhile, a surge in the number of immigrants made native-born white

Americans anxious about their own status. That April of 1896, on a visit to New York where he took up the current fad of bicycling, Kipling met "Red-Badge-of-Courage" Stephen Crane, as Carrie dubbed him. Both Kipling and Crane were searching for new models of heroism; there are parallels between Crane's battlefield courage and Kipling's courageous fishermen.

But *Captains Courageous* is more than a simple outward-bound tale of the toughening up of a spoiled rich boy. Missing from Kipling's summary to Elizabeth Ward is what one might call the "night side" of the novel, its evocation of dream and psychic inwardness, including the "second sight" ascribed to the sympathetically drawn African American cook. For what Harvey Cheyne receives aboard the *We're Here*, along with manual training and lessons in teamwork, is an education of the senses, of aesthetic sensibility. Manliness, for Kipling, required something more than mere discipline and duty. It is on the return trip of the *We're Here*, packed to capacity with iced cod, that Harvey learns to look at nature in a way other than the purely instrumental. "But since there was no fishing," Kipling writes, "Harvey had time to look at the sea from another point of view."

In a passage reminiscent of a series of Monet paintings—depicting a cathedral or a haystack in the differing light of dawn, midday, and dusk—Kipling allowed the ocean to teach young Harvey to look and to see. "The dullest of folk cannot see this kind of thing hour after hour through long days without noticing it," Kipling wrote, "and Harvey, being anything but dull, began to comprehend and enjoy the dry chorus of wave-tops turning over with a sound of incessant tearing; the hurry of the winds working across open spaces and herding the purple-blue cloud-shadows; the splendid upheaval of the red sunrise; the folding and packing away of the morning mists, wall after wall withdrawn across the white floors; the salty glare and blaze of noon; the kiss of rain falling over thousands of dead, flat square miles; the chilly blackening of everything at the day's end; and the million wrinkles of the sea under the moonlight, when the jib-boom solemnly poked at the low stars, and

Harvey went down to get a doughnut from the cook." The gently expanding metaphor of the white sheets, first tearing, then the glorious "folding and packing away of the morning mists, wall after wall withdrawn across the white floors," and finally wrinkled, holds the passage together right through to its domestic close.

At the same time that his eye is sensitized, Harvey gets an education of the ear. He lives aboard ship in a world of poetry—not of the high, literary variety but rather of words in rhythm and meter that match the physical rhythms of an active life at sea. There are hymns for lost sailors, humiliating rhymes directed at passing ships, and seagoing chanteys and ballads. One of the ballads built into the structure of the narrative, like a lyrical accompaniment, is John Greenleaf Whittier's "Skipper Ireson's Ride," once familiar to all educated New Englanders, and a popular text for public recitation. "Of all the rides since the birth of time, / Told in story or sung in rhyme," Whittier begins, "The strangest ride that ever was sped / Was Ireson's, out from Marblehead!" Ireson, as Whittier tells the story, was the captain of a fishing ship that foundered at sea, and who abandoned his crew on the doomed vessel in order to save himself. Kipling, who had already borrowed from Whittier's ballad the title of his gothic tale "The Strange Ride of Morrowbie Jukes," evidently wanted readers to associate his own sea yarn, *Captains Courageous,* with tales of old New England like Whittier's.

The reunion of Harvey Cheyne Jr. with his parents, after their mad dash across the American continent aboard Cheyne Sr.'s private railroad car, is the emotional high point of the novel, recalling Kipling's own railroad journey in 1889. Something unsettling enters the picture as Kipling contrasts the luxury of the private car with the less privileged lives of those outside in the engulfing darkness.

> At night the bunched electrics lit up that distressful palace of all the luxuries, and they fared sumptuously, swinging on through the emptiness of abject desolation. Now they heard the swish of a

water-tank, and the guttural voice of a Chinaman, the click-clink of hammers that tested the Krupp steel wheels, and the oath of a tramp chased off the rear-platform; now the solid crash of coal shot into the tender; and now a beating back of noises as they flew past a waiting train. Now they looked out into great abysses, a trestle purring beneath their tread, or up to rocks that barred out half the stars. Now scaur and ravine changed and rolled back to jagged mountains on the horizon's edge, and now broke into hills lower and lower, till at last came the true plains.

Kipling instills a cinematic immediacy into the racing train, punctuated by repetition of the word "now," like telegraph poles flitting past. It is easy to miss the hints—the tramp chased off the platform, the Chinese worker, the "abject desolation"—that all is not well in the heartland, with an economic depression wracking the country, outraged workers striking in major cities, and millionaires like Harvey Cheyne making obscene amounts of money in the unregulated businesses of railroads, mining, and timber.

5.

Trouble was brewing in Brattleboro as well, with Beatty Balestier, Kipling's wayward brother-in-law, the cause and catalyst. Accustomed to bailing out her wayward brother, Carrie decided, during the spring of 1896, that it was time for Beatty to learn a lesson. The Kiplings suggested a deal: they would assume the care of Beatty's young daughter if Beatty would dry out and get a job. Humiliated, Beatty feared that the Kiplings had designs on his property next to Naulakha. He also suspected that Rudyard, from his perch in the drugstore on Brattleboro's Main Street, had gossiped about Beatty's precarious financial situation.

And then things came abruptly and disastrously to a head. Kipling was out for a bicycle ride, his new passion, when he took a spill. At precisely that moment, Beatty, driving his carriage and roaring drunk, loomed into view and demanded a talk. "If you have anything to say, say it to my lawyer," Kipling replied. Beatty lost his temper. "By *****, this is no case for lawyers," he bellowed. "If you don't retract those ***** lies, I will punch the ***** soul out of you. I will give you a week in which to retract, and if you don't, I will blow your ***** brains out." Kipling filed a complaint through his lawyer, and Beatty was arrested for "assault with indecent and opprobrious names and epithets and threatening to kill."

So great was the interest of the Brattleboro townspeople, and then the national press, that the proceedings, set for May 12, were moved to the largest assembly room in the town hall. Meeting over drinks with reporters, Beatty framed the dispute as a comic standoff between a Falstaffian ruffian and a priggish killjoy. "This sounds serious and dangerous," wrote the reporter for the *Boston Daily Globe*, after Kipling had described Beatty's menacing behavior. "But when the manner of the speaker is jovial and even humorous, when he winks to bystanders and laughs at the jests of counsel, one gathers the impression of a consummate actor rehearsing his part in a farce comedy." The reporter's conclusion was devastating for an insecure man like Kipling. "There is a feeling here ... and notwithstanding the numerous debts which Beatty owes to local tradesmen, [that] he is the more manly man of the two."

Any hope for a prompt settlement was soon dashed. The judge issued a preliminary ruling in Kipling's favor, and demanded bail from Beatty if he wished to escape jail. When Beatty said he couldn't pay the bond, Kipling—adding another farcical detail to the circus—offered to do so. Beatty refused the gesture. After Beatty's lawyer posted the bond, the judge set the date for a second hearing in September. "Rud a total wreck," Carrie wrote in her diary. "Sleeps all the time. Dull, listless and weary. These are dark days for us."

At this grim juncture, yet another fishing trip was proposed. Kipling packed his rod and reel on June 15 and set off for the coast of Newfoundland, where he remained for two weeks. "It's a great land and I caught a 15-lb salmon—my first on the fly," he reported on July 2, "and I have grown three inches in my boots since." This time, Kipling's fishing companion was Lockwood de Forest, the New York designer who had helped decorate Naulakha. As the dreaded second judicial hearing approached, the Kiplings abruptly decided to leave Brattleboro, but they left open the possibility of a return. "I don't think quite of quitting the land permanently," Kipling wrote William Dean Howells. "It is hard to go from where one has raised one's kids and builded a wall and digged a well and planted a tree." His hurried departure to England, in late August, "was the hardest thing I had ever had to do," Kipling said. "There are only two places in the world where I want to live," he lamented, "Bombay and Brattleboro. And I can't live in either."

6.

The Kiplings spent their final night in a hotel near the Hoboken dock where their ship waited. Rudyard wrote a long letter to William James, the distinguished Harvard psychologist. With his wife, Alice, James had visited Naulakha in June 1895, just after the Kiplings had returned from Washington. He was tremendously impressed with Kipling, whom he compared to Shakespeare. William James has come to be known for the conviction that young people in peacetime needed a challenge comparable to battle—a "moral equivalent of war"—to learn the martial virtues of "intrepidity, contempt of softness, surrender of private interest, obedience to command." They needed danger, they needed hard physical labor, and they needed extreme experience to relieve their boredom amid prosperity. Kipling and James discussed precisely this theme a few years before James delivered his famous speech at Stanford (Harvey Cheyne's alma mater) on the moral equivalent of war. Kipling and James, it now seems clear, developed the idea together.

On August 31, the day before the Kiplings left the United States, Kipling wrote to say that *Captains Courageous* was the book that James had urged him to write. "I have just finished off a long tale wherein I have deliberately travelled on the lines you suggest—i.e., I have taken the detail of a laborious and dangerous trade (fishing on the Grand Banks) and used it for all the romance in sight." Kipling diagnosed the American predicament of the 1890s. "*Half* your trouble is the curse of America— sheer, hopeless well-ordered boredom; and that is going some day to [be the] curse of the world. The other races are still scuffling for their three meals a day. America's got 'em and now she doesn't know what she wants but is dimly realizing that extension lectures, hardwood floors, natural gas and trolley-cars don't fill the bill."

Reciprocally, Kipling's novel on deep-sea fishing, written along the lines that James had suggested, left an imprint on "The Moral Equivalent of War." "To coal and iron mines, to freight trains, to fishing fleets in December, to dishwashing, clothes-washing, and window-washing, to road-building and tunnel-making, to foundries and stoke-holes, and to the frames of skyscrapers," James proclaimed, "would our gilded youths be drafted off, according to their choice, to get the childishness knocked out of them, and to come back into society with healthier sympathies and soberer ideas." Indeed, the famous novel and the famous essay— with William James's prescription of "fishing fleets in December" to toughen up the "luxurious classes"—might be thought of as an imaginative collaboration between two writers bent on solving an American problem.

Chapter Ten

———

DHARMA BUMS

1.

"In a gloomy, windy autumn *Kim* came back to me with insistence," Kipling wrote in *Something of Myself*, recalling the long gestation of the strange and magical novel that he had begun in Vermont in 1892. He had put the manuscript aside several times before picking it up in earnest, six years later, during the summer of 1898. He and Carrie were living at the time in an old stone house in the isolated village of Rottingdean, four miles down the Sussex coast from the English seaside resort of Brighton. The Rottingdean village green, a mile inland from the sea, was anchored by North End House. This imposing structure served as a summer refuge, furnished by William Morris, for Sir Edward Burne-Jones and his wife, Georgiana, Kipling's favorite aunt. Originally two houses, North End House had a gap between its two connected structures that allowed huge canvases to be moved in and out. Nearby, there was another opening known as "the Gap," in the chalk cliffs of Rotting-dean, which gave access to a lovely valley and the rolling Sussex Downs beyond.

Over the years, Rottingdean had become a Macdonald family colony, a gathering place for relatives of Kipling's mother. Rudyard's cousin Stanley Baldwin had married a Rottingdean neighbor. Meanwhile, Lock-wood Kipling, in poor health, had retired from his position in India and settled with Alice in Tisbury, in Wiltshire, an easy train ride from Brighton. The proximity of family members gave the Kiplings abundant reason to settle down in the South of England as well. "Let the child that is coming to you be born in our house," the Burne-Joneses had generously urged the Kiplings. And so it was that John Kipling, their third child, was born in North End House on a warm August night in 1897.

Finding refuge in the Burne-Jones household, filled with art and exotic furniture—medieval love seats, heavy-legged tables, and a quaintly painted piano with green keys—recalled Kipling's difficult childhood years when he spent holidays with his uncle and aunt. Burne-Jones was collaborating with William Morris on their illuminated version of *The Aeneid*, and providing designs, known as "cartoons," for stained-glass windows. Burne-Jones was also painting *The Beguiling of Merlin*, in which so much depends on the play of the magician's shadowed blue eyes, as he is turned into a hawthorn bush by Nimue, the snake-haired Lady of the Lake. The half-finished pictures at the Grange in New York made a strong impression on Kipling. "At bedtime one hastened along the pathways, where unfinished cartoons lay along the walls," he wrote. "The Uncle often painted in their eyes first, leaving the rest in charcoal—a most effective presentation. Hence our speed to our own top-landing, where we could hang over the stairs and listen to the loveliest sound in the world—deep-voiced men laughing together over dinner." Now, Kipling himself had joined the deep-voiced men laughing over dinner, even as the memory of those eyes peering from the darkness stayed with him.

The Kiplings stayed on with the Burne-Joneses while looking for a house of their own. They ventured down the coast to Dorset, where Thomas Hardy showed Rudyard around on a bicycle. When a house called "the Elms"—"old, red-tiled, stucco-fronted with worm-eaten stairs"—opposite North End House became available, the Kiplings grabbed it. "It was small, none too well built, but cheap," Kipling noted, "and so suited us who still remembered a little affair at Yokohama." Kipling was recalling the banking disaster during their honeymoon, and the refuge they had found in tiny Bliss Cottage in Vermont. Shielded by high flint walls for privacy, the Elms had once served, Kipling learned, as "an old depot for smugglers." The novelist Angela Thirkell, grand-daughter of the Burne-Joneses, fondly recalled evenings when the visiting children would be invited into Kipling's bow-windowed study, and Kipling would read aloud from his *Just So Stories.* "There was a ritual about them," she remembered, "each phrase having its special intonation which had to be exactly the same each time and without which the stories were dried husks."

2.

When *Kim* first took root in Kipling's imagination, in Vermont, he envisioned a short story about an English child who helps a Tibetan lama find "a miraculous river that washed away all sin." The story mushroomed over the years, and Kim became an Irish child instead, "Kim o' the Rishti," dialect for "Kim of the Irish," with the initials *K* and *R* reversing Kipling's own. Once again, as with Mowgli among the wolves, or Harvey Cheyne between luxury liner and fishing boat, Kipling was exploring a central character caught between two worlds. He made frequent visits to Tisbury to go over Indian details of the story with his father. "Under our united tobaccos it grew like the Djinn released from the brass bottle," Kipling wrote, "and the more we explored its possibilities the more opulence of detail did we discover." Kipling found it hard to relinquish some of the riches, adopting a metaphor later used by Hemingway: "I do not know what proportion of an iceberg is below the water-line, but *Kim* as it finally appeared was about one-tenth of what the first lavish specification called for."

"Nakedly picaresque and plotless," in Kipling's assessment, *Kim* is a string of vivid encounters played out across northern India, as the boy and the priest search for the elusive river. In this twin search, Kim assumes the guise of Ananda, cousin and helper of the Buddha, or Enlightened One, embodied by the Tibetan lama. The search is a pilgrimage; the epigraphs to the first two chapters are drawn from Kipling's poem about the statue of the Buddha at Kamakura, a destination for pilgrims. Much of the book's energy and originality are derived from a second search, however: the quest for Kim's identity.

Kim's birth parents are a drunken Irish soldier named Kimball O'Hara and the unmarried English nursemaid whom he seduces. When the young mother dies, Kim's father takes up with a Eurasian prostitute. She introduces him to her own vice of opium, which kills him. Alone in the world, Kim owns nothing but an amulet around his neck, sewn by his father's lover. Inside are documents left to him by his father: his membership in a Masonic lodge, his regimental papers, and Kim's birth certificate.

There is one more bequest from Kim's father. The prostitute shares with him a mysterious prophecy. She informs Kim that he will recognize his destiny when he sees a red bull on a green field. Kim's quest eventually finds confirmation of the prophecy when he encounters the colors on the banner of his father's Irish regiment, the Mavericks. The vivid image of red and green exerts a larger gravitational pull on the narrative, however, encompassing both horoscopes and landscape details. In his efforts to decipher images, Kim finds a willing partner in the Tibetan lama. For the lama is himself a master of images, creating vivid representations, in a complex, calligraphic fusion of drawing and writing, of the Wheel of Life.

3.

Kim is a novel of education, with special attention to the proper training of the eyes. The narrative begins at the threshold of an art museum, a place consecrated to informed looking. Kim and his playmates clamber on the great cannon placed opposite the entrance. Kim sits, "in defiance of municipal orders, astride the gun Zam-Zammah on her brick platform opposite the old Ajaib-Gher—the Wonder House, as the natives call the Lahore Museum." It is there, by the museum, that Kim encounters the mysterious holy man, the Teshoo Lama, who has come on foot from Tibet and sought out the Wonder House as part of his own quest for the Buddha's sacred river.

The leisurely narrative allows us to consider what the museum might mean to the "keen-eyed" Kim and his devout companion, who "followed and halted amazed" in the entrance hall. The lama marvels at the spectacular Gandharan (i.e., Alexandrian) treasures on view. Kipling shows off his knowledge of these hybrid masterpieces of Buddhist and Greek inspiration, fashioned "by forgotten workmen whose hands were feeling, and not unskillfully, for the mysteriously transmitted Grecian touch." The lama's informed guide is the kindly curator or "Keeper of Images," modeled on Kipling's own father. The Keeper gives the lama a gift of crystal spectacles, the better to look at these Buddhist *stupas* (structures containing relics) and *viharas* (monastic halls).

Kim is adopted as the elderly lama's *chela*, his assistant and pupil, entrusted to beg food for him and provide for his comfort. But with his eager curiosity and shape-shifting talents for camouflage and mimicry, Kim is also drawn into the aims of other schemers, who turn out to be the English officers and their native spies of the British Raj in northern India. Kim delivers secret messages and outmaneuvers the Russian agents on the other side of the "Great Game" (a term Kipling made current) of imperial rivalry. When the kindly British officer Creighton recognizes Kim's extraordinary intelligence, he persuades the boy to enroll in a school, from which Kim periodically escapes to pursue his own adventures. Like the legendary native Pundits who, disguised as wandering priests, first surveyed the contested border regions dividing Afghanistan and India, Kim is trained to be a surveyor, a chainman, who can draw accurate maps and decipher them as well. He is himself a keeper of images.

4.

If the Lahore Museum is the first stage of Kim's education in looking, and his training as a surveyor his second, Lurgan Sahib's mysterious antique shop in Simla, the summer resort of the British colonial establishment in the Himalayan hills, is the culmination of his preparation. "The Lahore Museum was larger," Kim notes, "but here were more wonders" from all over the world. Kim sees "gilt figures of Buddha and little portable lacquer altars; Russian samovars with turquoises on the lid; egg-shell china sets in quaint octagonal cane boxes; yellow ivory crucifixes—from Japan of all places." But Lurgan himself is the strangest curiosity on view. "A black-bearded man, with a green shade over his eyes, sat at a table, and, one by one, with short, white hands, picked up globules of light from a tray before him, threaded them on a glancing silken string, and hummed to himself the while." The description zooms in on the jeweler's eyes. "He slid off the green shade and looked fixedly at Kim for a full half-minute. The pupils of the eye dilated and closed to pin-pricks, as if at will." With his elaborate memory games and illusionist tricks, Lurgan, with his "hawk's eye," systematically teaches Kim *how to look.* Eight times in the course of the Play of the Jewels and the other games, Lurgan commands Kim, simply and urgently: "Look!"

Like Kim's other masters of the Great Game, Lurgan is teaching Kim the skills required of a police spy. And yet this "healer of pearls" seems more a master of some esoteric Glass Bead Game ("The Glass Pearl Game" is the literal translation of Hermann Hesse's title) than an instructor in weaponry or the proper handling of state secrets. Lurgan's specialty is the art of repairing broken necklaces. This mysterious necklace mender is a master in discerning *how things are linked together.* This would seem to be an important skill for young spies to learn. It is at Lurgan's shop that Kim first meets another of his father-like masters, the Bengali Babu. Reinforcing the point that informed looking is the key to Kim's activities, the Babu teaches Kim the secret password for recognizing other players of the Great Game. Kim is instructed to bring the conversation around to specific curry dishes, including a vegetable curry known as *tarkeean.* Then he is to say, "There is no caste when men go to—look for *tarkeean.*" As the Babu carefully explains, "You stop a little between those words, 'to—look.' This is the whole secret." The whole secret, to put it differently, is to look.

As Kipling details the stages of Kim's apprenticeship, stringing episodes together to put Kim's lessons to the test, he is also inventing a new literary genre: the novel of international espionage. The narrative structure of the novel and its characters—the gifted secret agent, his training in spycraft and weaponry, his masters in the game, his disguises, his sinister rivals—will flower in the works of Eric Ambler and Graham Greene, Ian Fleming and John le Carré. At the same time, *Kim* may rightly be considered, as Hannah Arendt puts it, the "foundation legend" of the British Secret Intelligence Service, a narrative argument meant to justify the British presence in India.

And yet, as Arendt notes, the Great Game as portrayed in Kipling's novel is less a matter of political allegiance for Kim than it is the great adventure of life itself. "Since life itself ultimately has to be lived and loved for its own sake, adventure and love of the game for its own sake easily appear to be a most intensely human symbol of life." Kim relishes the diversity of modern India and refuses to take sides. "It is this underlying passionate humanity that makes *Kim* the only novel of the imperialist era in which a genuine brotherhood links together the 'higher and lower breeds,'" Arendt observes. "Kim, 'a Sahib and the son of a Sahib,' can rightly talk of 'us' when he talks of the 'chain-men all on one lead-rope.'" She notes that Kim's use of the collective "us" is "strange in the mouth of a believer in imperialism" like Kipling. And yet "playing the Great Game, a man may feel as though he lives the only life worth while because he has been stripped of everything which may still be considered to be accessory. Life itself seems to be left, in a fantastically intensified purity." It is this intensity of engagement with life, Arendt suggests, that brings readers back to *Kim*.

5.

The end of the search is marked by two epiphanies. The lama's discovery of the River of the Arrow is told rather than shown. The location of the river, which turns out to be a nondescript trickling brook, has come to him, like a cosmic reward, with his release from the things of this world. It is only when he has learned to renounce both his beloved native hills and his *chela*, his disciple Kim, that he can achieve the supreme detachment of enlightenment. Kim's own moment of enlightenment, by contrast, is shown rather than told, and involves a *reattachment* to the things of this world. Fittingly, Kim's nirvana is achieved by a higher act of looking, a seizing of the world made new after a spate of physical arduousness and fever.

As in "The Bridge-Builders," opium is the magic elixir that opens the doors of perception for Kim, in a moment of higher looking. "Then he looked upon the trees and the broad fields, with the thatched huts hidden among crops—looked with strange eyes unable to take up the size and proportion and use of things—stared for a still half-hour. All that while he felt, though he could not put it into words, that his soul was out of gear with his surroundings." Like a mantra, he repeats to himself the conundrum of personal identity: "I am Kim. I am Kim. And what is Kim?" The realization that follows is the emotional high point of the novel.

> He did not want to cry—had never felt less like crying in his life—but of a sudden easy, stupid tears trickled down his nose, and with an almost audible click he felt the wheels of his being lock up anew on the world without. Things that rode meaning-less on the eyeball an instant before slid into proper proportion. Roads were meant to be walked upon, houses to be lived in, cattle to be driven, fields to be tilled, and men and women to be talked to. They were all real and true—solidly planted upon the feet—perfectly comprehensible—clay of his clay, neither more nor less.

Two famous passages from Ralph Waldo Emerson undergird Kim's wondrous awakening. One is the ecstatic evocation, in *Nature*, of a per-fect attunement, or adjustment, between human consciousness and the natural world, as in Kim's feeling that the wheels of his being are locked up anew on the exterior world. Emerson's own version of nirvana swept over him as he walked across a village square. "Crossing a bare common, in snow puddles, at twilight, under a clouded sky . . . I have enjoyed a perfect exhilaration. I am glad to the brink of fear," he wrote. "Standing on the bare ground—my head bathed by the blithe air, and uplifted into infinite space—all mean egotism vanishes. I become a transparent eye-ball; I am nothing; I see all." The other passage that Kipling draws on is from Emerson's "Experience," written after the tragic death of his young son, and underwrites Kim's dawning awareness that "men and women [were meant] to be talked to. They were all real and true." Here, for comparison, is Emerson's original: "Five minutes of today are worth as much to me, as five minutes in the next millennium. Let us be poised, and wise, and our own, today. Let us treat the men and women well: treat them as if they were real: perhaps they are." The expansive spirit of Emerson's writings pervades Kipling's novel. Emerson's injunction that "Everything good is on the highway" could be the epigraph for *Kim*, in which the phrase "on the road" recurs throughout the novel.

6.

There is another classic work of American literature in the background of Kim's adventures. It seemed self-evident to Jorge Luis Borges that *Kim* was "written under the influence of Mark Twain's *Huckleberry Finn*." The two novels have many features in common. Kim and Huck share their adventures with older companions on purposeful journeys. The goal of the search, for both the mendicant lama and the escaped slave Jim, is freedom: freedom from "attachment" to the things of the world for the lama; freedom from slavery for Jim. Both the lama and Jim owe their liberation to their young companions, who are unimpaired by the prejudices of their elders. Kim saves the lama from all manner of threats, literally carrying him to his final destination, the River of the Arrow. Huck decides he would rather go to hell than betray Jim to slave hunters. Along the way, both Kim and Huck delight in shape-changing disguises, "passing"—like so many heroes of American fiction during the 1890s— for what they are not. "We come to understand the River by seeing it through the eyes of the Boy; but the Boy is also the spirit of the River," T. S. Eliot wrote of Twain's masterpiece. Kim's lama is in search of a river, to be sure, but the real counterpart of the Mississippi River in *Kim* is the Grand Trunk Road, "such a river of life," Kipling notes, "as nowhere else exists in the world."

Both novels are idylls shadowed by traumatic historical events. Told through the voice of a child, *Huckleberry Finn* soft-pedals the horrors of slavery, and cruelly plays, in its notorious closing chapters, with Jim's quest for freedom. *Kim* is set in the wake of the anti-British Revolt of 1857. An old veteran, a loyalist to the British colonial power, is allowed to interpret the meaning of the civil uprising as a "madness" that

Lockwood Kipling's bas-relief illustration of Kim and the lama, On the Road *(1901).*

descended on the native soldiers, resulting in the murder of English noncombatants in Lucknow, Delhi, and Simla—all sites visited in the course of *Kim*. An English guide would point out the sites of the "Mutiny" in Lucknow, we are told by the narrator—the House of the Ladies, for example, where English women and children were slaughtered. But Kipling invites us to see the city through Kim's eyes instead, its gleaming mosques catching the morning sun as it rises behind the bridges spanning the river.

Kim and *Huckleberry Finn* were to have a meeting of sorts. During the summer of 1895, following his visit to Washington, Kipling alerted friends that he planned to travel to India in the fall. He wanted to refresh his impressions in order to make progress with *Kim*. Twain was about to embark on a world tour of his own, lecturing to raise money to repay creditors after various get-rich-quick schemes had failed. Twain hoped that a reunion might be arranged in India, with Kipling guiding Twain around his favorite native haunts. About to board a ship in Vancouver, Twain fired off a letter to Kipling.

"It is reported that you are about to visit India," he wrote. "This has moved me to journey to that far country in order that I may unload from my conscience a debt long due to you." Twain remembered their first meeting. "Years ago you came from India to Elmira to visit me, as you said at the time. It has always been my purpose to return that visit and that great compliment some day." Then Twain unleashed a barrage of jokes, as though practicing for his upcoming lectures. "I shall arrive next January and you must be ready. I shall come riding my ayah with his tusks adorned with silver bells and ribbons and escorted by a troop of native howdahs richly clad and mounted upon a herd of wild bungalows; and you must be on hand with a few bottles of ghee, for I shall be thirsty."

The Indian reunion had to be called off when Carrie found herself pregnant. Kipling never did return to India, as it happened. But Twain traveled through India anyway. Schooled by Kipling, and drawing on the same English authority, Major General Sir William Henry Sleeman, whose tales of Indian children adopted by wolves had inspired *The Jungle Book*, Twain had nothing but admiration for the colonial rulers. "The handful of English in India govern the Indian myriads with apparent ease, and without discernable friction, through tact, training, and distinguished administrative ability, reinforced by just and liberal laws—and by keeping their word to the native whenever they give it." There is a striking passage in *Following the Equator* in which Twain, horrified by an incident in a Bombay hotel, is reminded of slavery in the American South. The hotelkeeper accompanies Twain and his family to their upper-floor room. There is some trouble with the door, and a native gets down on his knees to remove the impediment. "He seemed to be doing it well enough, but perhaps he wasn't, for the burly German put on a look that betrayed dissatisfaction, then without *explaining* what was wrong, gave the native a brisk cuff on the jaw and *then* told him what the defect was."

Twain was appalled, as forgotten events from his childhood flooded his memory. "I had not seen the like of this for fifty years," he wrote. "It carried me back to my boyhood, and flashed upon me the forgotten fact that this was the *usual* way of explaining one's desires to a slave." He remembered "that the method seemed right and natural to me in those days, I being born to it and unaware that elsewhere there were other methods; but I was also able to remember that those unresented cuffings made me sorry for the victim and ashamed for the punisher." Twain's father rarely lifted a hand against his own children, "yet every now and then he cuffed our harmless slave-boy, Lewis, for trifling little blunders and awkwardnesses." And then: "When I was ten years old I saw a man fling a lump of iron-ore at a slave-man in anger, for merely doing something awkwardly—as if that were a crime. It bounded from the man's skull, and the man fell and never spoke again. He was dead in an hour." Twain appears to draw a parallel in this passage between the abuses of the British Raj and the slaveholding South. And yet Twain never quite equates the English in India with the slaveholders in Missouri. He makes clear, more than once, that the abusive hotelkeeper in Bombay was German, not English, hence not a true administrator of the Raj. For Twain, the German bully is an intruder, an exception to the general order and good behavior of the ruling class.

Kim and *Huckleberry Finn* are uncomfortable reminders that blindness and insight are often oddly combined in our major writers. Mark Twain had nothing good to say about American Indians; Kipling was a great admirer, quick to condemn European settlers for genocide in the Americas. Both writers trafficked in racial stereotypes. The blatant stereotyping of Jim's character, in which the conventions of minstrelsy are invoked in speech and mannerisms, is matched in *Kim* by the repeated invocation of supposedly native traits, as when we are told that Kim lied "like an Oriental." And yet both books may be said to contain their own potential antidote. The hope of the future, in both, lies in the open eyes of children. "Look!" Kim is repeatedly told. Both novels imply that the jaded worlds of adult hatred and division can only be healed by new visions.

Chapter Eleven

———

WAR FEVER

1.

In late January 1899, Rudyard and Carrie Kipling began their return journey to the United States, a decade after Kipling had first set foot on the American continent. The traumatic events that had led to their abrupt departure from Vermont three years earlier had eased somewhat. The Venezuelan border dispute, which had opened a dangerous rift between the United States and Britain, had been resolved, in part through the zealous efforts of the Anglophile American ambassador John Hay, one of Kipling's friends from his Washington days. Beatty Balestier remained a volatile presence in Brattleboro. The main purpose of the trip was not a mission in family peacekeeping, however, but a reunion with Carrie's mother in New York, to introduce her to the newest member of the family, John, barely a year old. Another incentive for the trip was that Kipling was pleased with political developments in the United

States, and eager to take a closer look, or even to lend his voice if appropriate.

During the momentous summer of 1898, the United States had decisively entered the Great Game of empire building. Using the pretext of an explosion on the American battleship *Maine*, in Havana harbor, Americans helped liberate Cuba and Puerto Rico from Spanish rule. Extending the conflict into the Pacific, the United States also freed the Spanish colonies of Guam and the Philippines, while leaving open the question of what such freedom might mean to the inhabitants. Along the way, the United States also seized the previously independent country of Hawaii. Seemingly overnight, the United States had extended its borders beyond the North American continent, with the alluring prospect of new markets for its exports, new refueling ports for its ships, and new outposts of defense for its growing navy. A glorious future of American expansion was in view, as war fever swept the country.

President McKinley, a Civil War veteran of the killing fields of Antietam, was ambivalent about the national mania surrounding the pressing question of what to do about the Philippines. Should the United States grant the country independence or occupy it instead? An indigenous Filipino resistance movement was already well underway when Admiral Dewey attacked the Spanish fleet in Manila, and assurances of independence seemed—at least to the leader of the insurgents, Emilio Aguinaldo—to have been clearly expressed. But after a series of speeches around the country, McKinley claimed to have had an epiphany on an October night. Uncertain what to do, he went down on his knees and prayed for guidance. "I don't know how it was," he later reported. "But it came."

God had apparently informed the president that the Filipinos were "unfit for self-government" and that it was thus the duty of the Americans "to take them all, and to educate the Filipinos, and uplift and civilize and Christianize them and by God's grace do the very best we could by them, as our fellow men for whom Christ also died." He instructed

John Hay to inform the American negotiators that the entire Philippine archipelago should pass to American hands. As the Kiplings prepared for their departure, it remained uncertain whether the American Congress, divided between imperialists and their equally ardent foes, would ratify the Treaty of Paris and embrace occupation.

2.

Amid the "splendid little war"—as John Hay, named secretary of state in September 1898, famously called the conflict with Spain—a new national hero had emerged. Kipling's old friend Teddy Roosevelt had skillfully used every stage of the Spanish-American War to his advantage. Under the tutelage of Senator Henry Cabot Lodge, the leading voice of the imperialist faction, Roosevelt had pushed the cause of expansion at every opportunity. As assistant secretary of the navy, he had taken advantage of the momentary absence of his superior to give the order to Admiral Dewey to attack the Spanish fleet in Manila Harbor. He had resigned his position to lead the First United States Volunteer Cavalry, nicknamed the "Rough Riders," and achieved a glorious victory in the siege of San Juan Hill. Sporting his swashbuckling cavalry hat and armed with a pistol salvaged from the *Maine*, he managed to shoot a Spanish soldier. "He doubled up as neatly as a jackrabbit," Roosevelt boasted.

Anti-imperialists were predictably appalled. Roosevelt "gushes over war as the ideal condition of human society, for the manly strenuousness which it involves," wrote William James in disgust, "and treats peace as a condition of blubberlike and swollen ignobility, fit only for huckstering weaklings." James was invoking the very question that he had taken up with Kipling in Vermont: how to find some "equivalent" to war for inspiring American youth. But Roosevelt was given a hero's welcome on his return from Cuba. The only question, for the master manipulator Henry Cabot Lodge, was to chart his protégé's most efficient path to the presidency. A strategy was quickly adopted and flawlessly executed. Roosevelt was elected governor of New York in November 1898; two years later, he was selected as President McKinley's running mate, a heartbeat from the presidency, for his second term.

Kipling felt that he had a major stake in all these developments. Roosevelt, Hay, and Lodge were all personal friends of his. As an experienced hand in the Great Game, Kipling believed that he had lessons to impart to these fledgling players. "Now go in and put all your influence into hanging on permanently to the whole of the Philippines," he urged Roosevelt. The specific contribution that Kipling himself could make to the cause was an appropriate *language* for imperial ambition. On January 10, he wrote to his friend Robert Barr about his impending journey. "We're only going over for a month or six weeks—just to cheer up Teddy who is governor of New York and don't you forget it," he wrote. Then he added, "See next McClure's for a poem about expansion which will make you rejoice."

Kipling was referring to "The White Man's Burden," an explicit plea for the United States to adopt the Philippines as an American colony. The subtitle was "The United States and the Philippine Islands." Kipling believed that it was time for the United States to assume its share of the responsibilities of empire, previously carried by Great Britain: "Take up the White Man's burden—/ Send forth the best ye breed—/ Go bind your sons to exile / To serve your captives' need." Kipling argues that the imperialist impulse is strictly humanitarian, that it concerns a burden reluctantly assumed. The poem is silent on the two primary reasons why seizing the Philippines was so attractive to Americans. First, Filipinos would constitute a new market for American goods at a time when American industrial and agricultural production had outpaced American consumers. "With our protective tariff wall around the Philippine Islands," Lodge calculated, "its ten million inhabitants, as they advance in civilization, would have to buy our goods." And second, American warships would have a perfect base for patrolling the Pacific.

Self-pity is the dominant emotional note of "The White Man's Burden." For Kipling, the colonial powers will never be adequately thanked for all that they have selflessly accomplished for the natives, filling "full the mouth of Famine," and bidding "the sickness cease." Instead, "through all the thankless years," the imperialists will reap the "old reward": "The blame of those ye better, / The hate of those ye guard." Kipling sent the poem to Theodore Roosevelt, who, in a letter to Lodge, deemed it "good sense from the expansionist standpoint" but "rather poor poetry." Lodge replied, "I think it is better poetry than you say." He circulated copies among his fellow senators. The day after the poem appeared in print, the Senate voted as Kipling urged: to occupy the Philippines.

The title of the poem is unashamedly racist, of course. Filipinos are referred to as "your new-caught, sullen peoples," as though the American army was in the business of trapping wild game. And yet the challenge Kipling envisions for the technologically advanced nations—of introducing modern medicine, sanitation, and transportation to those less fortunate—is roughly the task that the United States has long professed. If you changed a few words and renamed the poem "The Burden of the Developed World," you might be describing some of the better intentions of American foreign policy. Roosevelt put the case for occupation and development more crudely. In a letter to Kipling, he dismissed "the jack-fools who seriously think that any group of pirates and head-hunters needs nothing but independence in order that it be turned forthwith into a dark-hued New England town meeting."

3.

The Kipling family arrived in New York on February 2, three days before the publication of "The White Man's Burden" in *The New York Tribune* and other newspapers. At the dock, they were mobbed by reporters, one of whom wrote, in doggerel, "The Mowgli-man we found the greatest pest, / For the bloomin' sod 'e wouldn't talk at all." All three children were suffering from colds caught on the North Atlantic. They settled into the Hotel Grenoble, on Seventh Avenue at Fifty-Sixth Street, to rest, recuperate, and hide from the press. But the colds did not get better. On February 20, Kipling himself, according to an entry in Carrie's diary, "feels dull and has fever in the night." Three days later, Josephine was so sick that it was determined that she should be moved— perhaps to distance her from the flock of reporters camped out at the hotel—to the home of Lockwood de Forest's sister, Julia, on East Thirty-Fifth Street.

The next few days were dire, with Kipling under the care of his brother-in-law Dr. Theodore Dunham and various nurses. Kipling's lungs were severely congested, and he raved in a feverish delirium. Meanwhile, Josephine seemed to rally. And then, abruptly, the roles were reversed. Kipling, at the Grenoble, was able to breathe freely and fell into such a deep sleep that the doctor initially feared he was in a coma. Josephine's condition, meanwhile, suddenly worsened. On March 6, to everyone's horror, Carrie and Rudyard's beloved American daughter died. She was eight years old. In order not to endanger Kipling's own recovery, news of the calamity was withheld from him. The weeks of convalescence that followed were grueling, both physically and emotionally, as Kipling tried to take up the strands of his life again. He couldn't bear even to speak the name of his lost daughter.

4.

The weeks of isolation meant that Kipling missed the drama following the publication of "The White Man's Burden." But he left another, stranger memorial to American war fever. As he slowly emerged from his illness, unaware of the dire danger Josephine was in, Kipling recalled his bizarre dreams and hallucinations. Eager to preserve a record of his mental chaos, he summoned a stenographer to his sickbed and recounted all that he had experienced as he lay, in danger of his life, in his room in the Hotel Grenoble. The stenographic record constitutes a surreal pendant to "The White Man's Burden," its unconscious underpinning. Theodore Roosevelt was a major inspiration for both.

The transcript of Kipling's delirium is an extraordinary document, fascinating both for what it reveals about Kipling's mental state at this pivotal life-and-death moment and for the fact that he preserved it. The overall plot of the six-page narrative, which shifts between past tense and a more immediate present, is a tale of relentless victimization, as self-pitying in its way as "The White Man's Burden," with Kipling himself as the hapless victim. It resembles, in striking ways, two of Kafka's best-known nightmares. Kipling's paranoid fantasy prefigures *The Trial*, and the prosecution of Josef K. for a crime that is never specified. It also shares features with "In the Penal Colony," in which the victim is held in restraints while a diabolical machine carves the judicial sentence directly into his body. Kipling's delirium begins with a false and Kafkaesque accusation. "I began by going upstairs to large, empty, marble rooms on top floor of Hotel Grenoble and there finding illustrated paper and newspaper clippings containing letters and correspondence from a New York girl, called—to the best of my recollection—Bailey or Brady—accusing me in great detail of having larked around with a great many girls both before and after marriage; letters couched in vilest personal style." These, Kipling concluded, "were calculated to make harm between wife and myself." The newspaper clippings recall Kipling's humiliating and widely publicized lawsuit with his brother-in-law Beatty, a name that resembles Bailey or Brady.

At this point a potential rescuer appears on the scene, none other than Theodore Roosevelt himself. "He informs me, with great concern, that Miss Bailey is really a well-wisher of mine and has a wonderful submarine boat which could take me and family in course of night or two to see Robert Louis Stevenson." But it soon becomes clear that Roosevelt is lying: he is actually "in the pay of Miss Bailey (or Brady) and New York society to be revenged on me for calling her opprobrious names." Instead of taking Kipling to Samoa, for the long-anticipated meeting with Stevenson, the submarine surfaces instead under the New York town hall, where Kipling is made to lie "on a black iron bed." At this point, Roosevelt confesses that he is in on the joke and "the nurses reveal themselves as lady reporters for the *New York Journal*." To amplify the public humiliation, Kipling is "brought out into the sunshine in the presence of some 80,000 people and then taken away and told that bail is refused." He is wearing nothing but a nightgown, with no undergarments.

It is said that Kafka read his stories aloud to his friends over drinks and laughed uproariously. It seems quite possible that Kipling thought his own delirious tale was also funny. As the narrative draws to a feverish close, futile rescue attempts follow Kipling's display before the crowd. Dr. Conland, his old friend, spirits him away in a "big railway" that takes him, "always lying down," through the Connecticut countryside, with surprising sights out the window. "I pass my sister, seeing her face for a moment." It is a poignant glimpse: the delirious brother face-to-face with the bipolar sister. He allows himself to wonder about his own mental equilibrium, "and for a long time I debate whether I am or am not insane because it occurs to me that all insane people have an idea that all their food is drugged and that they are under restraint and that people are after their money."

Kipling is then informed that there is a plot to lynch him "on account of my remarks about Miss Bailey." He finds momentary refuge hiding "with a negro family," presumably in danger of being lynched themselves. Then, he hides on a ship owned by the Rothschilds "or some firm of equal standing," presumably also Jewish, another surprising ally in his flight from the lynchers. Presiding over the entire account is the sinister and duplicitous figure of Teddy Roosevelt, the ringleader in Kipling's systematic humiliation. "I hated Theodore more intensely than I ever hated anyone," he recalled of the dream. "When it was found out that he had been in league with Miss Bailey and the rest of New York society to play this town hall trick on me, he could come to me and say: 'I am afraid you must not mind this. I could not help doing it,' and he would stick things into me. I am very polite to him, meaning later to kill him when I got well."

5.

What might explain this extraordinary hostility directed at Roosevelt? This was, after all, a moment of high promise for Roosevelt. He was leading the charge to expand the United States into the Pacific. Was Kipling having second thoughts about the blustering flag-bearer of American imperialism? One hint comes from a second poem that had its gestation at the same time as "The White Man's Burden." While "The White Man's Burden" is future-oriented, rallying another country to join in spreading civilization across an ungrateful world, "Recessional" looks ruefully backward. Composed as a prayer, it warns against arrogance and imperial overreach.

> God of our fathers, known of old,
> Lord of our far-flung battle-line,
> Beneath whose awful Hand we hold
> Dominion over palm and pine—
> Lord God of Hosts, be with us yet,
> Lest we forget—lest we forget!

For this hymn in honor of Queen Victoria's sixty years on the throne, Kipling again borrows from Emerson, whose couplet "And grant us dwellers with the pine / Dominion o'er the palm and vine" is artfully collapsed into "Dominion over palm and pine," suggesting the British Empire extending from Ceylon to Canada.

If Kipling groused about ungrateful natives in "The White Man's Burden," in "Recessional" he is anxious instead about the excesses of the imperial masters.

> Far-called, our navies melt away;
> On dune and headland sinks the fire:
> Lo, all our pomp of yesterday
> Is one with Nineveh and Tyre!
> Judge of the Nations spare us yet,
> Lest we forget—lest we forget!

Kipling is now willing to acknowledge that the imperialist impulse is not restricted to the selfless taking up of "burdens." He knows that the Great Game appeals to baser instincts as well. For leaders and their followers who, "drunk with sight of power," "loose wild tongues" in proud "boastings," Kipling feels nothing but disgust and foreboding. He concludes: "For frantic boast and foolish word—/ Thy Mercy on Thy People, Lord!" Sending the poem to the London *Times* on July 16, 1897, he explained, "we've been blowing the Trumpets of the New Moon a little too much for White Men, and it's about time we sobered down." Despite its warnings, the poem was immensely popular from the moment of publication and sealed Kipling's reputation as the Laureate of Empire. John Hay summed up the reaction on both sides of imperial question: "It has touched everybody—not merely the critical people—as the one utterance of the year worthwhile."

But might the poem have had other implications, other targets, as well? Kipling had always regarded Americans as boastful and reckless, like the monkeys of *The Jungle Book* who fail to observe the Law of the Jungle. It has often been assumed that the "lesser breeds without the Law" referred to in the poem are the nonwhite races, but the allusion is actually to Saint Paul's "Gentiles, which have not the law," in the Epistle to the Romans. In early 1899, Theodore Roosevelt was building his

reputation on his boastful charge up San Juan Hill, winning the gover-
norship of New York and already looking, inevitably, to the presidency.
Is it possible that unstoppable Roosevelt came to seem—to a delirious
Kipling unable to control his conscious admiration for his obstreperous
young friend—a cautionary tale and, even worse, a potential menace?

6.

Kipling returned to England mostly recovered in body but not in spirit.
Even friends with differing political views rallied around him. Charles
Eliot Norton, a leader in the anti-imperialist movement, was attentive
through Kipling's illness and its aftermath; Norton's daughter, Sally, sat
by Kipling's bed and held his hand during the excruciating days after
Josephine's death. Another prominent anti-imperialist, Andrew Carnegie, offered his estate in Scotland during Kipling's convalescence, which
the Kiplings gratefully accepted, even as Kipling quipped to Carnegie
that he was eager to convert him to imperialism. Meanwhile, those closest to Kipling could see that something had changed in his emotional
world. "Much of the beloved Cousin Ruddy of our childhood died with
Josephine," Angela Thirkell noted. "There was the same charm, the
same gift of fascinating speech, the same way of making everyone with
whom he talks show their most interesting side, but one was only allowed to see these things from the other side of a barrier."

    We are given a glimpse of the other side in a passage from Kipling's
Just So Stories written after Josephine's death, and in her honor. In "How
the Alphabet Was Made," the alphabet is revealed as the big secret of the
world, but there are secrets of another kind concealed in the story. These
hidden meanings center on the sequence of letters *J-K-L*, and their re-
ordering in Kipling's alphabet necklace. The letter *K* in particular, "the
scratchy, hurty Ka-sound," is in the wrong place. But why "hurty"? Ulrich Knoepflmacher is surely right in suggesting that the hurt inscribed

in "How the Alphabet Was Made" is the death of Josephine. In the necklace that takes Tegumai five years to make, as though registering five years of mourning, the letters are in the sequence *J-L-K*, with this explanation:

> J is a fish-hook in mother-of-pearl.
> L is the broken spear in silver. (K ought to follow J, of course;
>   but the necklace was broken once and they mended it
>   wrong.)
> K is a thin slice of bone scratched and rubbed in black.

Following the "hurty" death of Josephine, whose name begins with *J*, the broken necklace is partially mended like a broken heart. Kipling, in mourning, is like "a thin slice of bone scratched and rubbed in black." The broken spear of *L* adds to the breakage, which includes the mother's pain as well, in the hook of mother-of-pearl.

Two beautiful verse elegies for Josephine-Taffy frame "How the Alphabet Was Made." The first associates her death with the vanishing wildlife along the Wagai River, when "beavers built in Broadstonebrook / And made a swamp where Bramley stands." The other poem pictures Taffy as Pocahontas, "in moccasins and deer-skin cloak," followed—as *K* should follow *J*—by her grief-stricken father:

> For far—oh, very far behind,
> So far she cannot call to him,
> Comes Tegumai alone to find
> The daughter that was all to him.

Josephine's death also meant the death of something else: Kipling's decade-long engagement with the United States. To his American friend Ted Hill, he was finally able to say something about what the devastating loss had meant to him. "I don't think it likely that I shall ever come back to America," he wrote in July. "My little Maid loved it dearly (she was almost entirely American in her ways of thinking and looking at things) and it was in New York that we lost her. Everybody was more than kind to us and to her but I don't think I could face the look of the city again without her."

Chapter Twelve

———

THE FLOODED BROOK

I.

Rakishly arrayed in his "surpassingly becoming" scarlet gown, silver-maned Mark Twain relished the procession through the Oxford streets. Those destined for honorary degrees from the famous university, that summer evening in June 1907, marched "between solid walls of the populace," Twain reported, "very much hurrah'd and limitlessly kodacked." It was an impressive lineup: the French composer Saint-Saëns, the sculptor Rodin, among other celebrated artists and scientists. Walking immediately behind Twain was Rudyard Kipling. Neither writer had ever attended college. From All Souls, they made their stately way to the Sheldonian Theatre, amid a shower of applause.

They arrived at the theater walking two by two, as Kipling noted in a letter to his son, John, and were herded into an antechamber. There, the doctors of literature and science were informed, they would have to

Mark Twain (left) *and Kipling* (right) *at Oxford, 1907.*

wait. "And we waited, and we waited, *and* we waited," Kipling wrote. Mark Twain asked, in a loud voice, "if a person might smoke here and not get shot." A horrified official responded, "Not *here!*" and gestured to an alcove. "So we went out," Kipling reported, "and Mark Twain came with us and three or four other men followed and we had a smoke like naughty boys, under a big archway."

It was a reunion of sorts, this gaggle of boisterous boys out of sight of the adoring public. Almost twenty years had elapsed since the first time that Kipling and Twain had chatted amid a cloud of cigar smoke, discussing the limits of autobiographical truth-telling and a possible sequel to *The Adventures of Tom Sawyer.* Since that first meeting in Elmira, Kipling and Twain, the undisputed literary lions of the English language, had remained acutely aware of one another, even as their careers sharply diverged, like mirror images of one another. Twain watched

Kipling's fortunes rise as his own declined, the result of ill-fated invest-
ment schemes and hurried writing. Kipling had settled in New England
even as Twain was leaving it. Kipling gave up restlessly circling the
globe just as Mark Twain began his own travels, retracing itineraries
that Kipling had taken long before him.

2.

For Kipling, the years from 1899 to 1914 were a time of rewards and fairies, to borrow the title of one of his books from the period. What he called
his "notoriety" had never been higher, both for the fame that he had won
from his writing and for the controversy that surrounded his increasingly
reactionary political opinions. A flood of honors was gratefully received
or gracefully refused, according to Kipling's determination to remain, at
all costs, a free agent in his writing. The laureateship, repeatedly offered,
was out of the question, nor would he consider, despite invitations, serving in Parliament. That fiercely protected freedom to follow the wayward
inner promptings of what he referred to as his Daemon was exploited in
the views he expressed—sometimes prophetically, in the elevated key of
"Recessional," and sometimes with extraordinary vulgarity. He alienated
many friends and admirers with his jingoistic support for English colo-
nialists in the Boer War in South Africa; in the lead-up to the Great War,
he urged the British to resist German expansion at whatever cost, warning, "The Hun is at the gate!"

Kipling's lungs had been permanently damaged from the pneumonia
he contracted in New York in 1899; doctors urged him to seek, henceforth, a warmer climate for the winter months. He had visited South
Africa for the first time the previous year, and returned with regularity
like a migratory bird. There, he developed an intense affection for the
English settlers and their leaders: Dr. Jameson of the quixotic raid
against the Dutch Boers, Alfred Milner, and, above all, Cecil Rhodes,

the imposing imperialist who built a rustic house for Kipling's personal use. Kipling adopted the British cause in South Africa, as he explained in *Something of Myself.* When Rhodes asked him, "What's your dream?" Kipling answered, swooningly, that Rhodes "was part of it." The Dutch he regarded with scorn, as mere pretenders to civilization, or worse. As for black Africans, who had a far greater right to the land than either colonial power, Kipling barely noticed their existence.

Amid his strident, and increasingly repellent, engagement with global politics, these were years of intense private mourning for Kipling. With Josephine's death, the United States had become a haunted place in his mind, never to be revisited except in the oblique approaches of his stories and verses, and in encounters with emissaries from his lost youth, like Mark Twain or Charles Eliot Norton. He found solace in travel, both in the annual family voyages to the British settlement in Cape Town—a "Paradise" for seven years, in Kipling's view, before the Boers regained control of the country—and in motoring around the Sussex countryside in his new passion, an automobile.

But the travel that increasingly preoccupied his days and nights was a deeper plunge into the storied past. He pored over archeological accounts of the South of England, brooding on Viking raiders and stalwart Roman centurions, the counterparts of the tough-minded soldiers he had known on the Indian border. He found spiritual anchorage in the odes of Horace, the torture of his school days and the joy of his disillusioned maturity. "Do not inquire what unseen end the gods have in mind for you," Horace had written. "Cut back far-reaching hopes and pluck the day"—*carpe diem.* Kipling painstakingly illuminated the margins of his Horace volumes with illustrations from his own lost worlds: American Indian peace pipes in memory of Bill Phillips, mosques from Lahore.

To native fairy tales, both freely adapted from original sources or invented from his own imaginative storehouse, he brought some of the same narrative vigor that he had applied to Mowgli's adventures. He found relief from his emotional turmoil in composing two time-traveling volumes, *Puck of Pook's Hill* and *Rewards and Fairies*. In these fairy realms, Kipling could mourn his losses in private. In public—to accept an illustrious award, to take part in an official commission, or to urge a political position in hammering verse—he remained firmly in control emotionally, with the iron resolution that he so admired in men like Theodore Roosevelt and Cecil Rhodes.

3.

Twain had also made his way to South Africa, traveling down from India. His qualms about Cecil Rhodes, Kipling's hero, were not enough to make him sympathetic to the Boers, and certainly not enough for him to embrace anything like self-governance for black South Africans. And yet, unlike Kipling, Twain thought the Boer War was ill-advised, and he was shocked in particular by the ineptness of Dr. Jameson's Raid, which Kipling regarded with some of the same reverence Northerners in the United States accorded John Brown's raid on Harpers Ferry. If their views on South Africa differed on tactics, however, Twain still supported the British.

It was after the Spanish-American War that the two writers' views on empire diverged most sharply. Twain had endorsed the war as long as he could persuade himself that the United States was fighting for the liberation of Cuba. But when Americans attacked the Filipino rebels they had pretended to defend, Twain's support ended in outrage. He fiercely opposed the American occupation of the Philippines, which he considered a betrayal of all that the United States stood for, since its own adoption of the Declaration of Independence. Kipling, by contrast, not only supported the invasion at the outset, but continued to take an interest in the oppressive American regime there.

And yet Twain's admiration for "my splendid Kipling," as he called him, endured. In August 1906, a year before the celebration at Oxford,

Twain noticed a Kipling poem in the morning papers attacking a new British policy in South Africa. The Liberal Party had regained leadership in the British Parliament, and voted for self-rule in the South African territories, effectively returning control to the majority (at least the white majority) Boers. In an intemperate poem titled "South Africa," Kipling equated the decision with the enslavement of the British settlers in South Africa. "At a great price you loosed the yoke / 'Neath which our brethren lay," he addressed the British people. "Our rulers jugglingly devise / To sell them back again." Kipling, who never reprinted the poem in any of his collections of verse, evidently came to feel that he had gone too far. But instead of criticizing Kipling's repugnant political views, Twain sought to excuse them, ascribing Kipling's love for "power & authority & Kingship" to "his training that makes him cling to his early beliefs."

4.

During the fall of 1907, after playing second fiddle to Mark Twain at Oxford, the Kiplings were invited to Canada for what amounted to a triumphal transcontinental tour, with a luxurious private railroad car for their enjoyment. What Kipling saw of Canadians persuaded him that this British dominion (as the colonies were called) was infinitely more civilized than its neighbor to the south. He marveled, in *Something of Myself*, "that on one side of an imaginary line should be Safety, Law, Honor, and Obedience, and on the other frank, brutal decivilization." Still grieving over the death of Josephine, Kipling refused to travel across the border. Mrs. Balestier was forced to make the journey from Brattleboro to Montreal to see her daughter and son-in-law.

On his return to England, Kipling was stunned to learn that he had been awarded the Nobel Prize. He was the first writer in English to win the award and, at forty-one, the youngest. His account of the occasion in *Something of Myself* is in stark contrast to the frolic at Oxford earlier that year. The king of Sweden died during the Kiplings' stormy voyage across the North Sea. Instead of the scarlet pomp of Oxford, the occasion in Stockholm, as Kipling described it, was a Whistlerian symphony in black and white.

> We reached the city, snow-white under sun, to find all the world in evening dress, the official mourning, which is curiously impressive. Next afternoon, the prize-winners were taken to be presented to the new King. Winter darkness in those latitudes falls at three o'clock, and it was snowing. One half of the vast acreage of the Palace sat in darkness, for there lay the dead King's body. We were conveyed along interminable corridors looking out into black quadrangles, where snow whitened the cloaks of the sentries.

Kipling decided that it must be from their native land that the hard-working Swedes drew their strength. "Snow and frost are no bad nurses," he reflected. Having endured many harsh winters of their own, the Kiplings now turned their attention to putting down roots in their newly adopted northern land.

Kipling had found a house in the Sussex countryside where he hoped that his family could recover some of the life that they had treasured in Vermont: isolation, privacy, a landscape fit for livestock, hard work, and stories. Naulakha had finally been sold in 1904. The house on the crest of a Vermont hillside had been on the market for several years, an unwelcome reminder of Josephine's death and the quarrel with Beatty. "I feel now that I shall never cross the Atlantic again," Kipling had written his old friend, Dr. Conland, in January 1903, "all I desire now is to get rid of *Naulakha* for $5000." Even the fire-sale price, sharply down from an initial offering of $30,000, was only feasible because members of the Cabot family mercifully took the house off his hands.

Henceforth, all things in Kipling's life revolved around Bateman's, the ironmonger's house that he had discovered on one of his roving tours of the countryside. The house itself, without electricity or running water when Kipling bought it, dated from the sixteenth century. The River Dudwell, meandering quietly through the meadows, had once powered a small mill near the house. Earlier still, a forge had been established in Roman times; plows and hoes turned up fragments of pig iron and ax-heads. Kipling consulted with Aurel Stein, the great archeologist and associate of Lockwood in Lahore, about his findings, and his sense that he was living atop an archeological hoard.

These layers of history sparked Kipling's imagination for *Puck of Pook's Hill* and its sequel, *Rewards and Fairies,* in which a brother and sister, Dan and Una, modeled on John and Elsie Kipling, are introduced to the previous denizens of the Weald, the clay-rich fields and woods of rural Sussex. The books feature some of Kipling's finest poems, including lyrical masterpieces like "Harp Song of the Dane Women" and "The Way Through the Woods." Burne-Jones supplied the original imaginative direction of these books. Kipling had asked him about possible historical sources, and Uncle Ned had asked historians like Mommsen, the German chronicler of ancient Rome. But he had also seen a way forward in Kipling's "'The Finest Story in the World,'" a tale that demonstrated, Burne-Jones wrote, "what the public might look for in your treatment of an ancient subject."

Again, Kipling turned to Longfellow, the inspiration for "'The Finest Story.'" Reading a volume of Longfellow serves as a charm for Una and Dan, by means of which they summon a sailor familiar with Viking longboats. In "The Knights of the Joyous Venture," the third tale in *Puck of Pook's Hill,* Dan reads aloud from Longfellow's "The Discoverer of the North Cape," and elicits a parallel story from an English sailor kidnapped by a Danish vessel. The story is preceded by Kipling's great seafaring poem in the Old English rhythm, "Harp Song of the Dane Women": "What is a woman that you forsake her, / And the hearth-fire and the home-acre, / To go with the old grey Widow-maker?"

A master theme running through the stories collected in *Rewards and Fairies* is the nature of human responsibility. In tale after tale, Kipling places the main character in difficult circumstances where a choice must be made despite imperfect options. A recurring question is "What else could I have done?" It is the question voiced by George Washington in a pair of tales set in eighteenth-century Philadelphia, a city Kipling remembered from his 1889 travels. Set in 1793, "Brother Square-Toes" celebrates the Anglo-American alliance that Kipling had long cherished. A Sussex boy named Pharaoh Lee, son of a Rottingdean smuggler, suffers the fate of Harvey Cheyne when a French warship, in thick fog, runs down the dinghy in which he and his father are retrieving barrels smuggled from relatives in France. Pharaoh becomes a cabin boy on the warship transporting the French ambassador, Genet, to Philadelphia. Genet's mission is to persuade George Washington to fight on the side of revolutionary France against Great Britain. Pharaoh apprentices himself in Philadelphia to a Moravian apothecary who trades with Seneca Indians in the Pennsylvania outback; they call the boy "Brother Square-Toes" for the prints that his shoes leave in the dirt.

Pharaoh accompanies two Seneca chiefs to Genet's meeting with President Washington, called "Big Hand" by the Indians. Washington firmly rejects the French appeal, despite American opinion running ten-to-one against the British. "Deal with facts, not fancies," he says, well aware that America, with no navy or army to speak of, is not equipped for another war. "Let me assure you that the treaty with Great Britain will be made though every city in the Union burn me in effigy," he insists. When Big Hand finishes his ringing speech, "it was like a still in the woods after a storm."

"Brother Square-Toes" is immediately followed, as an epilogue illustrating and enlarging the story, by Kipling's great poem "If—." Story and poem praise the immovable man, unswayed by public opinion, whether praise or blame. Kipling invites us to see Washington as the quintessential embodiment of the steely resolve described in the poem.

Familiar lines from the poem assume a fresh meaning when they are associated with President Washington, who refused the title of king: "If you can talk with crowds and keep your virtue, / Or walk with Kings— nor lose the common touch. . . ." Kipling finds his ideal of public comportment in an American leader, and in an American setting.

5.

A prominent feature of the extensive Bateman's grounds, and of the two Puck books, was a bubbling brook called Dudwell, at the foot of the garden, charmingly picturesque in most seasons but given to ruinous flooding without notice. "The waters shall not reckon twice / For any work of man's device," Kipling wrote in "The Floods." The brook became an idiosyncratic character in his life and his fiction, as lively and unpredictable as any of his friends or neighbors. It became, indeed, something like the spirit of the place itself, to be loved and treasured but also, as a local deity, feared and propitiated. Drainage was a constant challenge. "We've been fighting floods in our valley—putting in pipes and drains and trying to persuade our innocent looking little brook that it isn't a Colorado river—so far without success," Kipling wrote in 1911.

Kipling compared his own efforts to control the not-so-innocent brook with the industry of his beloved beavers. "Except for three days of light snow-powder every hour has been usable in the open and we've worked like beavers cutting wood, putting in great water-drains under roads, setting up fences, hauling faggots etc. etc.; always with one eye on our Rogue River—the innocent brook that has already flooded us once this year," he wrote, before enlarging the comparison.

> I suppose God gave us superfluous energy the same way he gave the Beaver incisors that have to grow; and for fear our mental incisors should end by growing on and on and curving back and

piercing our brains, he invented the whole generation of stubborn, ox-eyed, mule-hearted, mud-footed farmers in lieu of the Beaver's wood stumps. So we all run about chewing and biting and carrying mud in our forepaws ... and slapping our tails to the greater glory of God and, I hope, the advantage of the land.

The brook at the foot of the garden inspired, in its seasonal permutations, some of Kipling's most vivid stories during his English years. "'My Son's Wife'" strands a progressive young urbanite named Midmore in a country estate inherited from a deceased aunt. At first, the land—with its stubborn old tenant farmer named Sidney, its house too close to a "dull, steel-colored brook," and its foxhunting neighbors—seems a burden, to be sold off as soon as possible. Midmore is dismayed to learn from his local lawyer, Sperrit, that the property is encumbered by various liens, nor is it worth as much as he had hoped. "The repairs are rather a large item—owing to the brook," says the classically trained lawyer. "I call it Liris—out of Horace, you know." The ode alluded to asks what the poet wants from Apollo, and answers, "not an estate which is gnawed by the Liris, that silent river, with its gentle stream."

As his name suggests, Midmore, like so many of Kipling's characters, is caught between two worlds. The twin tasks of repairing the farm and riding to the hounds awaken feelings in himself that he had been unaware of. The brook is the anarchic wild force in the story. When it floods to record levels, it dredges up one love story from the deep past (Sidney and Midmore's loyal housekeeper, Rhoda) and stirs up another in the present (Midmore and Connie Sperrit, daughter of Midmore's Horace-quoting lawyer, and an avid horsewoman). The flood is a Darwinian test, dividing the fit from the unfit: "Now what is weak will surely go, / And what is strong must prove it so."

6.

A favorite escape for Kipling, amid all the work on the Bateman's property, was motoring around with his car and driver—he never drove himself—in the Sussex countryside. He paid visits to Henry James, who lived nearby, and other neighborhood acquaintances. But if driving was a distraction, from his work and his losses, it was also ghost-ridden. The car as a vehicle of time travel and the death of Josephine are united in one of Kipling's greatest achievements, the eerie ghost story titled "They."

The narrator is a grieving father. On a pleasant drive in early summer, he finds himself "clean out of my known marks." He passes through a village named Washington, "which stands godmother to the capital of the United States." At a crossroads, amid the "confusing veils of the woods," he has no idea which road to take. He stops to ask for directions at an "ancient house of lichened and weatherworn stone." The tenant, a blind woman, seems somehow aware of his own loss. He notices children looking out from the upper windows. "Oh, lucky you!" the woman cries, apparently, he assumes, because she is unable to see them, but actually, as he soon learns, because they are visible to him. The children shy away from the narrator's approach, vanishing into the underbrush outside or the shadows within. On a second visit, the car itself seems to know the way to the dilapidated house in the woods.

"They" is structured like a detective story, in which the identity of the children is concealed from the grieving narrator even as the reader gradually surmises the true state of affairs. The moment of revelation comes only on the third visit, amid falling leaves at summer's end. Having tea with the blind woman, the narrator is again aware of children hidden in the shadows, shyly keeping their distance like scared animals. As a way to build their trust, he pretends to be unaware of them, "when I felt my relaxed hand taken and turned softly between the soft hands of a child." The gesture was a "mute code" devised between father and living child "as the all-faithful half-reproachful signal of a waiting child not used to neglect even when grown-ups were busiest."

"Then I knew," says the narrator. The blind woman, he realizes, is a medium with psychic powers, capable of calling up ghosts from the spirit world. The house in which she lives is haunted by the ghosts of dead children, who can be summoned into the presence of those mourning their deaths. This reunion across the barrier of death is immediately followed by the narrator's firm decision never to return to the haunted house. "For me it would be wrong," the narrator tells the blind seer, wrong to trespass on the sacred precincts of the dead.

7.

Kipling's resolve to close the portals of the dead was tested again at the outset of the Great War. His only son, John, was not yet seventeen. Like his father, Jack, as he was known, had bad eyes, but he was determined to join in the war effort. Rejected for an officer's commission, he tried to enlist as a private instead, again without success. His father pulled strings and Jack was enrolled as a junior officer in the Irish Guards. On his first day of battle, almost his first hour, at the hideous arena of mechanical warfare amid the trenches of Loos, in Belgium, Jack was reported missing, presumably blown to pieces by a German shell. No remnant of his body was ever recovered.

After the war, Kipling accepted a position on the Imperial War Graves Commission, charged with honoring the memory of the war dead. In this capacity, he traveled often to France and composed the official inscription on the British graves. He also wrote, in a less official vein, the darkly moving "Epitaphs of the War," in which he left far behind the saber-rattling jingoism of his prewar verses. "Who dies if England lives?" he had asked at the outset of the war. In his heartbreaking elegy for Jack, with its prevailing metaphor of a wreck at sea, he gave the answer.

"Have you news of my boy Jack?"
Not this tide.
"When d'you think that he'll come back?"
Not with this wind blowing, and this tide.
"Has any one else had word of him?"
Not this tide.
For what is sunk will hardly swim,
Not with this wind blowing, and this tide.

For two years, Jack remained officially missing, but Kipling knew differently. "The wife is standing it wonderfully tho' she, of course, clings to the bare hope of his being a prisoner," Kipling confided to a former classmate serving in the army. "I've seen what shells can do, and I don't." Predictably, spiritualists wrote to Kipling promising to put him in touch with his lost son. A visit from Trix, deep in her own clairvoyant fantasies, augmented his frustration. "I have seen too much evil and sorrow and wreck of good minds on the road to Endor," he wrote in *Something of Myself,* alluding to a sorceress in the Book of Samuel, "to take one step along that perilous track." He put his objections into verse in the wartime poem "En-Dor," in which he acknowledged the temptation: "Whispers shall comfort us out of the dark—/ Hands—ah, God!—that we knew!"

8.

And then, unexpectedly, someone touched Kipling's arm again, touched it not once but twice. It began with a dream.

I dreamt that I stood, in my best clothes, which I do not wear as a rule, one in a line of similarly habited men, in some vast hall, floored with rough-jointed stone slabs. Opposite me, the width of the hall, was another line of persons and the impression of a crowd behind them. On my left some ceremony was taking place that I wanted to see, but could not unless I stepped out of my line because the fat stomach of my neighbor on my left barred my vision. At the ceremony's close, both lines of spectators broke up and moved forward and met, and the great space filled with people. Then a man came up behind me, slipped his hand beneath my arm, and said: "I want a word with you."

A few weeks later, Kipling attended a ceremony at Westminster Abbey, in his official capacity as a member of the Imperial War Graves Commission. The Prince of Wales was there to dedicate a plaque in honor of the million dead in the Great War.

We Commissioners lined up facing, across the width of the Abbey Nave, more members of the Ministry and a big body of the public behind them, all in black clothes. I could see nothing of the ceremony because the stomach of the man on my left barred my vision. Then, my eye was caught by the cracks of the stone flooring, and I said to myself: "But here is where I have been!" We broke up, both lines flowed forward and met, and the Nave filled with a crowd, through which a man came up and slipped his hand upon my arm saying: "I want a word with you, please."

What Kipling describes is a striking example of what the Society for Psychical Research referred to as a "predictive dream." Mark Twain had also had such a dream when he and his brother, Henry, were training to be riverboat captains. Twain dreamed in great detail that his younger brother's body, draped with white roses and a single red one, was placed in a casket balanced across two chairs. So vivid was the dream that when Twain awoke, he was relieved to find his brother alive and well. Three days later, Henry was killed in a steamboat explosion. Twain hurried to the scene to find his brother in a metal casket, balanced between two chairs. "A volunteer nurse stepped up to the coffin and gently laid across it a bouquet of white roses with a single red bloom in their midst." Twain joined the Society for Psychical Research on the basis of the dream.

Kipling was wary of such moments of apparent clairvoyance. "For the sake of the 'weaker brethren'—and sisters—I made no use of the experience," he wrote, alluding, it would seem, to his own sister. It wasn't that he didn't believe in such occult events. The point was that he *did* believe in their reality, and in their danger. Of his own predictive dream, he allowed himself only one comment, and he put it in the form of a question. "But how, and why, had I been shown an unreleased roll of my life-film?" It is a striking metaphor. Kipling, who was intensely interested in the new technology of motion pictures, imagines each human life as a spool of film unrolling over time. On certain occasions, and without explanation, the ordinary chronological deployment is violated, and we are given a momentary glimpse of the future or the past.

Kipling, as it happened, was given access to both the past and the future as he stood, first in dream and then in reality, in the vast hall with the cracks in the stone floor. The ceremony at Westminster Abbey was emotionally overloaded for him. He was a commissioner of war graves, but he was also the grieving father of one of the million dead. Who exactly was the stranger in the crowd, who slipped his hand under Kipling's arm and said, "I want a word with you, please"? Could he be anyone other than an emissary from the land of the dead? This stranger repeats the gesture of the shy daughter in "They," who takes her grieving father by the hand. It is also the gesture of the lost son in "En-dor": "Hands— ah, God!—that we knew!"

The dream of Westminster Abbey was to be doubly predictive, as Kipling surely knew. For even as he was hurriedly writing *Something of Myself,* Kipling was certain that he himself did not have long to live, and that death would soon take him by the hand and ask to have a word with him. As the most celebrated English writer of his age, Kipling could be confident that his own last reward would be a memorial in Westminster Abbey. And so it was that when he died, just after his seventieth birthday, his ashes were buried in Poets Corner, alongside the graves of Chaucer and Tennyson. The funeral service was held amid a great crowd in the vast hall with the cracked stone floor.

American Hustle

I.

During the Vietnam War, when it began to dawn on many Americans that what the British had experienced in India and Afghanistan might also apply to them, Kipling's work took on new relevance. A stray phrase from a little known Kipling poem—initially quoted as "you cannot hurry the East"—wormed its way into the very highest levels of decision-making. The phrase was invoked, repeatedly, during the perilous start of the war, at a time when many options, including American withdrawal, were still in place. The making of key decisions turned on the proper interpretation of Kipling's ambiguous phrase—indeed, on the meaning of a single word. The same phrase, at war's end, seemed to have predicted the whole debacle from the beginning.

But Kipling had not, in fact, used the word "hurry," as journalists discovered when they finally took the trouble to look up the wording of the original. He had warned instead against any attempt to *hustle* the East.

> And the end of the fight is a tombstone white with the name
>   of the late deceased,
> And the epitaph drear: "A Fool lies here who tried to hustle
>   the East."

The poem warns against any attempt to meddle in the affairs of a distant country. It is, one might say, the antidote to "The White Man's Burden," another poem often invoked in discussions of Vietnam. During the Vietnam War, Kipling's little poem about folly in the East was quoted and misquoted by saber-rattling generals and antiwar journalists alike. The question of precisely how the poem was to be interpreted resembles, in key ways, the proper historical interpretation of the war in Vietnam (and of subsequent wars in Afghanistan, Iraq, and Syria that have come to resemble it in unsettling ways).

History may not repeat itself, at least not in any exact sense, but it does sometimes seem to view itself in a distorting mirror. "Those who remember the past are condemned to repeat it too," as Michael Herr wrote of Vietnam. Many participants compared the Vietnam War with the "splendid little war" (in John Hay's phrase) that the United States fought with Spain in 1898. Some of the major decision-makers of the Vietnam War had familiar names, including Henry Cabot Lodge, grandson of the Massachusetts senator, and Kim Roosevelt, grandson of Theodore, which gives the moment of crisis during the early 1960s an eerie aura of déjà vu. The CIA operative who initiated and orchestrated American involvement in the conflict came straight from the Philippines, the ambiguous prize of the Spanish-American War, and regarded *Kim* as his playbook. And whether these Americans hurried or hustled the Vietnamese remains a point of contention among historians and politicians.

2.

Among the classic Vietnam memoirs, Philip Caputo's *A Rumor of War*, recording the experience of the very first marines to see combat there, best captures this uncanny sense of historical recurrence. "It was a peculiar period in Vietnam, with something of the romantic flavor of Kipling's colonial wars," Caputo writes. He recalls how Lieutenant Bradley, an officer for the battalion, "perfectly expressed the atmosphere of those weeks. He called it the 'splendid little war.'" Caputo places his reader doubly in Kipling country: in the world of late Victorian colonial outposts, in *Kim* or "Mandalay," and in the Spanish-American War of 1898. For Caputo and his fellow soldiers, the romantic flavor would end soon enough, as would any splendor. "It was not so splendid for the Vietnamese," as Caputo adds dryly.

As the combat intensified, and the savage search-and-destroy missions in the Vietnamese jungles brought no discernible progress in the war, it was a different side of Kipling's work that seemed more relevant: the bleak poems of the ordinary soldier's life in the *Barrack-Room Ballads*. These poems detailed the daily humiliations and sudden violence among the enlisted men, while the officer class exuded arrogance and incompetence. Caputo's soldiers know their Kipling by heart; preparing for combat, a fellow soldier recites, "I'm old and I'm nervous and cast from the service," from Kipling's bitter home-front ballad "Shillin' a Day." For Caputo, Kipling's iconic British soldier, Tommy Atkins—hard-drinking, loyal to his mates in combat, humiliated on the home front—could just as well have been an American marine. "Most American soldiers in Vietnam—at least the ones I knew—could not be divided into good men and bad," Caputo writes. "I saw men who behaved with great compassion toward the Vietnamese one day and then burned down a village the next. They were, as Kipling wrote of his Tommy Atkins, neither saints 'nor blackguards too / But single men in barricks most remarkable like you.'"

3.

During the summer of 1963, two years before Lieutenant Caputo and his fellow marines arrived, there was still a good deal of disagreement among American decision-makers, civilian and military, about what the precise role of the United States should be in the future of Vietnam. No country named South Vietnam was recognized in the Geneva agreements that ended French occupation in 1954. But President Kennedy's advisers were leery of potential Chinese influence in Southeast Asia, and—on the analogy of Germany and Korea—considered a divided Vietnam a better outcome than the prospect of a wholly Communist one. This early period of indecision was to be the romantic, swashbuckling phase of the conflict, as Caputo described it. It is difficult to avoid the impression that the Americans involved thought they were playing a stylish game, even a new version of the Great Game.

Not surprisingly, it was Kipling's *Kim* that served as a semiofficial code of conduct. CIA operatives were instructed to read the novel. It is not an exaggeration to say that from 1954 on, the Vietnam War was fought—at least from the covert American viewpoint—according to Kipling rules. *Kim* was the first modern novel of international espionage, so it is hardly surprising that real-life spies should have found it so useful, so confirming. But the status of the novel in the CIA was more specific, more precise, more exalted than mere entertainment literature. For just as *Kim* had inspired Lord Baden-Powell in structuring the Boy Scouts, an organization intended to prepare British youngsters for the rigors of military service, CIA chiefs combed Kipling's novel for lessons to train another gallant brotherhood.

The initial impetus came from Kermit Roosevelt Jr., a grandson of Theodore Roosevelt, who was nicknamed Kim at an early age. Kim Roosevelt's father, serving with British forces in World War I before the

United States entered the war, had visited Kipling at his country estate at Bateman's, and raised his son in the Kipling ethos. Kim Roosevelt was a legendary figure in the early years of the agency, and bestowed a taste for *Kim* on his fellow operatives. A well-thumbed copy of Kipling's novel was found at the bedside of Allen Dulles, an early director of the CIA, at his death.

But the man who most firmly imposed the picaresque spirit of *Kim* on the mushrooming conflict in Vietnam, and who issued directives and planned missions according to the actions of Kimball O'Hara, was Edward G. Lansdale, the first architect of American strategy in the region. Lansdale was held in high regard for what he was seen to have accomplished in the Philippines, liberated (once again, after the debacle of 1899) by American troops, this time from Japanese occupation. Lansdale's operatives had successfully undermined Communist influence in the archipelago and helped to empower a regime sympathetic to the United States. They had done so by means of military and technological aid, and through efforts to reach the "hearts and minds" of the people via a sophisticated propaganda campaign. Surely, Lansdale was the man, it was widely believed, to accomplish something comparable in Vietnam, in the wake of the French failure to wrest the country from Communist control. Lansdale, it was hoped, might at least shore up a South Vietnam friendly to American interests while weakening the Communist nationalist Ho Chi Minh's hold on the North.

In June 1954, Lansdale arrived in Saigon as the official head of the military mission there and, covertly, as the station chief for the CIA. For the next two years, Lansdale pursued three main initiatives. One was to organize teams to carry out secret operations in the North, sabotaging transportation hubs in Hanoi and coordinating other acts of terrorism. A second initiative was to encourage anti-communist Catholics in the North to immigrate south. And third, Lansdale scouted out the possible leaders among the competing private armies and local strongmen of

Saigon and its surroundings and settled on Ngo Dinh Diem—a mandarin with close ties to American Catholics—as the right man to lead South Vietnam and work closely with the Americans.

What united this complicated portfolio, in Lansdale's mind, was the inspiring figure of Rudyard Kipling. "Vietnam was so filled with the arcane," he wrote in his memoir, "that I used to advise Americans to read Kipling's '*Kim*' and pay heed to the description of young Kimball O'Hara's counterintelligence training in awareness of illusions." The scene in which Lurgan Sahib trains Kim to remember elaborate patterns of jewels had also been the starting point of Baden-Powell's romance with the novel. Now, Lurgan's game was used to train American operatives doing dirty tricks in North Vietnam.

4.

On the recommendation of Lansdale, the United States decided to bet on the Catholic President Diem. President Kennedy took over where the French had left off, helping to outfit and train Diem's ARVN troops. The general in charge of what was euphemistically called the Military Assistance Command was General Paul D. Harkins. Harkins had served under George Patton during World War II, where he earned the nickname "Ramrod" for his determination to keep his troops moving forward. An accomplished polo player at West Point, Harkins saw Vietnam as an old-fashioned military theater, in which iron resoluteness would win the day and impress the home-front audience. Harkins looked the part and, in fact, played minor roles in war movies. He was also, like Lansdale, a Kipling enthusiast. Harkins "misquoted Kipling in a sardonic remark" directed to the chairman of the Joint Chiefs of Staff, according to historian Stanley Karnow. "You can't hurry the East," Harkins insisted.

Harkins's warning about the dangers of undue "hurry" was leveled principally against his main rival in Saigon, Henry Cabot Lodge Jr.,

President Kennedy's choice as American ambassador. Nixon's running mate in 1960 and a former United States senator from Massachusetts, Lodge was the father of George Cabot Lodge, who, as a young naval lieutenant, had accepted the surrender of the city of Ponce in Puerto Rico in 1898. A promising poet, George Cabot Lodge had died young and was elegized in a short biography by Henry Adams, a gift for his friend Henry Cabot Lodge Jr., the young poet's father and the leading American imperialist of his time.

Ambassador Lodge was impatient with the lack of progress on the part of the South Vietnamese government in suppressing the Communist rebels, the Vietcong. He was particularly impatient with President Diem, whom he considered insufficiently resolute, as well as divisive in his oppression of Buddhists in South Vietnam. Photographs and television footage of elderly Buddhist monks lighting themselves on fire in the streets of Saigon stunned American viewers and angered Kennedy. Lodge had had enough of Diem. When he learned of plans by a disgruntled group of Vietnamese generals to stage a coup against Diem, he was eager to throw American support—covertly, of course, through the CIA—behind the plan.

Harkins strongly opposed the coup. On August 31, 1963, he sent a top secret telegram to General Maxwell Taylor of the Joint Chiefs of Staff, in Washington, and requested that copies be shared with the secretary of state and the head of the CIA. A note on the document, made public in the Pentagon Papers, shows that President Kennedy also read it. The main point of Harkins's telegram was that the South Vietnamese generals disagreed about the coup. "So we see," he concluded, "we have an 'organization de confusion' with everyone suspicious of everyone else and none desiring to take any positive action as of right now." Harkins then added, as though clinching the argument, "You can't hurry the east."

Harkins's warning, borrowed from Kipling, fell on deaf ears. President Kennedy and his advisers agreed not to thwart the coup, a reassurance duly conveyed to the conspirators. On November 1, news reached

Washington of the success of the coup, although Kennedy was alarmed to learn that Diem had been murdered rather than escorted abroad. Deceived by the generals with the promise of safe passage, he had been summarily shot in the head instead. Lodge congratulated the generals in his office and triumphantly cabled President Kennedy: "The prospects now are for a shorter war."

Three weeks later, President Kennedy was assassinated. Despite his ongoing friction with Ambassador Lodge, General Harkins remained in charge of military operations for another year. He continued to claim, against the skepticism of some American reporters on the scene, that progress was being made on the battlefield. For his tendency to inflate body counts of killed Vietcong, Harkins came to be known by members of the press as "General Blimp" (after the cartoon character Colonel Blimp). Looking for fresh leadership, President Johnson, in 1964, appointed William Westmoreland, Harkins's second-in-command, to replace him as head of combat troops in Vietnam. Dean Rusk, Johnson's secretary of state, emphasized the urgent need to "change the pace at which these [Vietnamese] people move." Harkins duly warned Westmoreland against undue haste, misquoting Kipling yet again about the danger of hurrying the East. But hurry remained, for the moment, the first order of business, as Westmoreland expanded—or "escalated"—the war. Westmoreland followed Harkins's lead in reporting progress, as defined by body counts and "kill ratios." On a visit to the home front in November 1967, Westmoreland reported confidently that "the end begins to come into view."

And then, seemingly out of nowhere, came the stunning Tet Offensive, beginning the night of January 30, 1968, when Vietcong and North Vietnamese troops launched a massive and coordinated attack on many cities in the South, and stormed the American embassy in Saigon. The attack caught the American leadership by surprise, and inspired a good deal of second-guessing of Westmoreland's blithe assurances. Had he merely underestimated the troop strength of the opposition? Or had he, as some CIA insiders and journalists claimed, deliberately manipulated the numbers? Was the U.S. leadership the victim of an intelligence failure, or was it the perpetrator of a hoax? Had Westmoreland been guilty of undue *hurry* in bragging about the impending end of the war, or was he guilty, instead, of deliberately *hustling* the American people, as a controversial CBS documentary called *The Vietnam Deception* claimed?

5.

During the military escalation in Vietnam, someone had taken the trouble to look up the original wording of Kipling's poem, with the word "hustle" replacing the word "hurry." A reporter for *Time,* in an article dated May 24, 1964, reported that the Kipling poem was "much quoted in Vietnam by Americans who are desperately trying to hustle Premier Nguyen Khanh's regime into stepped-up action against the ever more aggressive Red guerrillas." Three years later, Robert Sherrod wrote in *Life,* "To change any Oriental's way of thinking—or, as Kipling put it, to hustle the East—is a major undertaking." But the work that most firmly conjoined the Kipling passage with the Vietnamese "quagmire"—the word that Mark Twain had first given its modern military meaning, in a remark about the American occupation of the Philippines—was again Caputo's *A Rumor of War.*

Caputo had been in Vietnam long enough to experience the decisive shift from low-key American military "assistance," which he had likened to Kipling's romantic colonial wars, to arduous engagement in combat operations, where he found resonances elsewhere in Kipling's work. Caputo describes a scene in which a fellow soldier creates an unwelcome distraction. "I am trying to read the paperback Kipling which lies open in my lap," he writes, "but I cannot concentrate because Gordon is talking and because an invincible weariness prevents me from reading more than a few lines at a time." Caputo intuits a connection here between

Kipling's work and Vietnam, but he can't quite grasp it, can't quite make it out. The print is smudged with his own sweat; Gordon's chatter distracts him from the meaning of the words on the page. Exasperated, Caputo interrupts Gordon's monologue by reading aloud from a poem that has caught his eye:

> And the end of the fight is a tombstone white with the name
> of the late deceased,
> And the epitaph drear: "A Fool lies here who tried to hustle
> the East."

Gordon, he notes, "misses the irony."

6.

But how exactly did Rudyard Kipling intend the irony? Did he mean "hurry" when he wrote "hustle"? For a passage that has so thoroughly worked its way into the fabric of recent American history, it is worth returning to the original source, and recalling that Kipling, too, was thinking about the problematic role of the United States in world affairs when he first wrote his little poem about hustling the East. During the winter of 1892, Kipling had just lost his best friend, Wolcott Balestier, and had almost immediately married Balestier's sister. He was aboard the *Teutonic* as it made its way across the bleak and frigid North Atlantic, on the first leg of his honeymoon. Henry Adams—the American historian, Washington insider, and enthusiast of American empire—was also aboard, and joined the Kipling wedding party for dinner each evening in the stateroom.

To while away the time, Kipling composed verses to serve as chapter headings for *The Naulahka*, the boisterous "Story of East and West" on which he and Wolcott Balestier had collaborated. The novel was built on the sort of plot—combining romance, the trade in valuable antiquities, and international intrigue—that was hugely popular during the 1890s, as the United States began to exert a role in international affairs. The American hero of *The Naulahka*, the mining engineer Nicholas Tarvin from the small town of Topaz, Colorado, arrives in India at the start of Chapter 5, and is immediately baffled by primitive travel arrangements, dubious telegraph connections, and government bureaucracy. He must learn to be patient if he is to achieve his objectives. It was for this chapter that Kipling wrote his four-line epigraph, using the same rollicking rhythm of his "Ballad of East and West" of 1889, with its famous opening, "Oh, East is East, and West is West, and never the twain shall meet":

> Now it is not good for the Christian's health to hustle the
>   Aryan brown,
> For the Christian riles, and the Aryan smiles and he
>   weareth the Christian down;
> And the end of the fight is a tombstone white with the name
>   of the late deceased,
> And the epitaph drear: "A Fool lies here who tried to hustle
>   the East."

The reader can easily discern the immediate referents of the poem. Tarvin is the Christian. His shifty hosts are the Aryans. He had better be patient and watch his step.

Tarvin is in India to hustle the local Maharaja out of his valuable necklace. He is also eager to hustle Kate, the Topaz woman he hopes to marry, out of her determination to have a life of her own. While Kate toils in a local hospital, with unspeakable sanitary conditions and a woeful lack of medical supplies, Tarvin proposes the construction of a new dam for the Maharaja, which will divert water from supposedly gold-rich sands. Kate and Tarvin seem to embody (at least for Kipling) the best tendencies of the White Man's Burden: promotion of public health and aid in the exploitation, through modern technology, of natural resources.

But the dam project is a ruse, a hustle, to beguile and distract the Maharaja. Tarvin knows perfectly well that there is no local gold to be found. What he wants is access to the Maharaja and, through him, to the necklace. Complications ensue. The Maharaja has taken a new wife, the seductive Sitabhai, who wants, in turn, to have her nine-year-old stepson killed so that her own child will be heir to the throne. When Tarvin tries to foil her murderous scheme, she lies about the location of the Naulakha necklace, directing him to an abandoned temple equipped with a sandstone trapdoor and a crocodile—details later adopted by the Indiana Jones movie franchise. Armed with the knowledge that Sitabhai is gradually poisoning her stepson, Tarvin proposes a deal: he won't expose her to the Maharaja if she gives him the valuable necklace. Appalled at such an underhanded deal, Kate insists that Tarvin return his ill-gotten gain. But such is the chaos at the hospital, where local religious extremists have accused Kate of poisoning their children, that Kate agrees to return to Topaz, where Tarvin's mines have recently—oh, happy day!—struck it rich. He has his fortune, and his bride, after all.

So, what about that dire warning concerning the tombstone white with its epitaph drear? Tarvin certainly did try to "hustle the East." There can be no doubt about that. Did he learn his lesson in the nick of time? Did Kate save the day? And finally, did Kipling mean "hurry" when he wrote "hustle"? There are many references in *The Naulahka* to the slowness of the East, beginning with Tarvin's frustrated efforts to reach the remote Indian state where his two prizes, Kate and the priceless necklace, are to be found. "In an hour the bullock-cart went two and a half miles. Fortunes had been made and lost in Topaz—happy Topaz!— while the cart ploughed its way across a red-hot river bed." And a few pages later: "This was plainly not a country in which business could be done at red heat." Tarvin learns that the best way to strike a good deal on travel arrangements is to claim, deadpan, "I'm in no hurry." In India, if you're in a hurry you need to pretend that you're not. In other words, you need to hustle a little.

The notion of hustling as involving deception is present at the origin of the English word, derived from a Dutch verb for shaking coins or lots in a hat. By 1800, "hustle" was already used for thieves jostling a mark, and later, by extension, for pool sharks, as in Paul Newman's 1971 movie *The Hustler.* The alternative meaning of pushing or hurrying is a later, and subsidiary, usage. And why wouldn't Kipling have used the word "hurry" if he meant hurry? When Paul Harkins quoted Kipling as saying you can't *hurry* the East, he was interpreting the word "hustle" in a plausible but not necessarily accurate way. It is more likely—and in fact, given the context in *The Naulahka,* fairly certain—that Kipling actually meant that you cannot *cheat* or *deceive* the East. Since Harkins himself was accused of deception in his optimistic body counts and sunny outlook on American progress during the Vietnam War, his suppression of the word has an unintended irony.

7.

By the mid-1970s, when the United States had finally unshackled itself from the conflict in Vietnam, the notion of American deception in the war had taken a firm grip on the country's imagination. Kipling is invoked in several Vietnam-related films. In the final segment of *Apocalypse Now* (1979), Dennis Hopper plays a fast-talking photojournalist who leads Captain Willard (Martin Sheen) to meet the unhinged imperialist Colonel Kurtz (Marlon Brando). Amid a manic flood of praise, Hopper calls Kurtz "a poet-warrior in the classic sense," adding, by way of illustration:

> And suddenly he'll grab you, and he'll throw you in a corner, and
> he'll say "Do you know that 'if' is the middle word in life? 'If you

can keep your head when all about you are losing theirs and blaming it on you, if you can trust yourself when all men doubt you . . .'"

Kurtz, in director Coppola's (and screenwriter Michael Herr's) view, is yet another fool who tried to hustle the East.

John Huston's *The Man Who Would Be King* is a more explicit engagement with imperial overreach and folly. The film appeared in 1975, the year of the fall of Saigon, and Huston let it be known that it had "contemporary significance." He had planned to film Kipling's dark tale for a long time; the ragged end of the American adventure in Vietnam added poignancy, and urgency, to the project. It is the story of two former British soldiers in India, Dravot and Carnehan, played by Sean Connery and Michael Caine. Dissatisfied with their military service in the Raj, which they consider unfit for lusty adventurers like themselves, they have become cynical con men instead. The devious pair make money by impersonating journalists and blackmailing Indian royalty with threats of embarrassing revelations in the press. Aiming higher, they come to grief in their scheme to hustle the kingdom of Kafiristan—across the Khyber Pass in what is now Afghanistan—of its treasure dating back to the time of Alexander the Great.

The film opens amid the chaos of a bazaar in northern India, as the camera roams from a blacksmith to vendors, blind beggars, snake charmers, and magicians. Then, as night falls, we are standing outside the lamp-lit windows of the *Northern Star* newspaper, as a stranger limps toward the door. Inside is Kipling himself, played by Christopher Plummer, writing a poem in blue ink. We can see that he is writing the opening lines of "The Ballad of Boh Da Thone" from *Barrack-Room Ballads*: "Boh Da Thone was a warrior bold: / His sword and his rifle were bossed with gold, // And the Peacock Banner his henchmen bore / As still with bullion, but stiffer with gore." A gruesome episode of guerrilla warfare in Burma, told with an unsettling humor, the poem ends with the severed head of the terrorist leader delivered to a retired British officer.

"I read so much Kipling, it's in my unconscious," John Huston once remarked. "You start a verse, I'll finish it." Huston expects us to know that "The Ballad of Boh Da Thone," with its jungle setting more closely matching Vietnam than the mountains of Afghanistan, has several elements in common with "The Man Who Would Be King," including a crucifixion, a severed head (the only "loot" brought back from these dismal wars), comic brio, and the presence of antiwar journalists ("While over the water the papers cried, / 'The patriot fights for his countryside!'"). Philip Caputo quotes a passage from the same Kipling ballad as an epigraph to one of the later chapters in *A Rumor of War*: "The worn white soldiers in Khaki dress, / Who tramped through the jungle and camped in the byre, / Who died in the swamp and were tombed in the mire."

In Huston's film, the battered man opens the office door and interrupts Kipling's work. "I've come back," he says. "Give me a drink, Rudyard Kipling. Don't you know me?" Kipling remembers, in a flashback, how he first met Carnehan, who stole his watch at a railroad station only to return it when, a Mason himself, he discovered a Masonic charm hanging from its gold chain. He asks Kipling, as a fellow Mason, to convey a message to Dravot, concerning their plans for an empire of their own in Kafiristan. Later, Carnehan and Dravot blithely explain their scheme to Kipling: they will help a local king defeat his enemies, take over his kingdom themselves, then take the loot and leave in triumph. When "Peachy" Carnehan returns from his ordeal, he has been reduced to a human shadow—crawling, starving, demented—and, evidently, tortured. (He has, in fact, suffered crucifixion, and carries Dravot's severed head in a bag.) He recounts a ghastly tale of the rise and fall of two fools who tried to hustle the East.

What gives the film its unsettling resonance with Vietnam—and with later American wars in Afghanistan and Iraq—is how breezily confident these confidence men are in their prospects for success. After all, they have modern weaponry (twenty Martini rifles); the natives have bows and arrows. When Dravot, protected by a concealed amulet, survives an arrow aimed at his heart, the natives take him for a god; when the Masonic emblem on the amulet matches their own age-old symbols, they take him for the divine son of Alexander himself. But when a bite from his reluctant child bride draws blood, revealing that he is human after all, the natives exact a horrifying price. The two would-be imperialists' facile scheme and grisly fate recall a line from Michael Herr's *Dispatches*: "There is a point of view that says that the United States got involved in the Vietnam War, commitments and interests aside, simply because we thought it would be easy."

Many scenes from the film and many individual lines, have a resonance beyond their ostensible narrative purposes. When Dravot tells a local leader, with broad irony, that he and Carnehan are "bringing enlightenment to the darker regions of the earth," it's a laugh line. In the extended scenes of military drill, the two ex-soldiers, resembling American advisers in Vietnam, train local men to fight like a modern army. "We're going to teach you soldiering," Dravot assures them, so they can "slaughter ... enemies like civilized men." When a battle is interrupted by a procession of holy men dressed in white, we almost expect them to set themselves on fire, like Buddhist monks in Saigon. Dravot and Carnehan manipulate their puppet ruler as cynically as the United States shuffled its designated leaders in Saigon, and suffer as ignominious a final defeat.

Among the many ironies of *The Man Who Would Be King* for American viewers today is its setting in Afghanistan, where American soldiers continue to die in the longest war in American history. The so-called "lesson of Vietnam," often invoked in relation to later American military excursions, apparently remains unlearned—indeed, not even fully formulated. "The war is over," Caputo writes in the prologue to *A Rumor of War*. "We lost it, and no amount of objecting will resurrect the men who died, without redeeming anything, on calvaries like Hamburger Hill and the Rockpile." He adds, "It might, perhaps, prevent the next generation from being crucified in the next war. But I don't think so."

What does it mean to say that Kipling has mapped out this territory already? Why do his poems and stories, written so long ago, seem so accurately to capture the experience of soldiers and officers in these dismal wars? Is it the tragedy that each period must make its own mistakes, even if they are the same age-old mistakes? Does the United States in Vietnam (or Iraq or Afghanistan) simply repeat the British mistake in India, or South Africa? Is this "the horror" that Kipling and Conrad so deftly discerned amid all the patriotic bluster, the sheer extremity of folly far from home? Emerson said that our moods do not know one another. Do our historical periods not know one another either? Now that the crucifixion Caputo feared has occurred, and not once but multiple times, is the unlearned lesson the same old banal one—that history repeats itself? Or is there some specific illness—call it imperialism—that Kipling had his finger on? What note did he hit, exactly?

8.

A few years after the ignoble and extremely hurried American retreat from Saigon, the reporter Michael Maclear interviewed General Westmoreland for his 1981 documentary of the war. At the end of an episode titled "Westy's War," Westmoreland recalls the handoff of power from General Harkins, in 1965, when Westmoreland was put in charge of military operations. According to Westmoreland, Harkins's habitual optimism about the war would suddenly darken, as he "constantly" quoted "a version" of a Kipling poem:

> The end of the fight is a tombstone white, with the name of
>   the late deceased.
> And the epitaph drear, "A fool lies here who tried to hustle
>   the East."

Deadpan, book in hand, Westmoreland reads the poem aloud, hesitating slightly over the word "drear," as though either its meaning or its placement—following rather than preceding the word "epitaph"—is puzzling to him. "I'm very fond of Kipling because he's a soldier's poet," Westmoreland concludes, staring straight into the camera. "I didn't take it quite to heart."

And so it was that Rudyard Kipling's work, as though to mark the centennial of his birth, was invoked to make sense of the war in Vietnam in three different phases. First, there was the buoyant (and boyish) romantic phase, when Edward Lansdale considered *Kim* the best possible guide for American escapades in Vietnam. This was the period, from 1954 up through the Diem coup, when the war seemed a second Great Game, in which CIA agents pulled off daring missions redolent of the Boy Scouts, to advance what they thought was the unimpeachable cause against the spread of Communism. The second phase was a dawning realism, when the body counts—and body bags—began to accumulate, and the clear-eyed view of ordinary soldiers in Kipling's *Barrack-Room Ballads* seemed a better gauge of the horrific quagmire that was emerging in full view on the televised evening news.

The third and final phase was the tragic realization that it had all been a terrible mistake, and on a truly colossal, even apocalyptic, scale, a folly of proportions still not fully known or adequately acknowledged, casting a long shadow on every subsequent decision by the United States in diplomacy and in combat. Here, too, Kipling had found precisely the right words for the debacle. After the death of his own son on the battlefield, a century ago, he wrote in *"Epitaphs of the War,"* adopting the voice of the dead:

> If any question why we died,
> Tell them, because our fathers lied.

ACKNOWLEDGMENTS

First of all, I am profoundly grateful to the National Endowment for the Humanities for granting me a Public Scholar Award for the 2016–17 academic year. Jon Western, dean of faculty at Mount Holyoke College, made it possible for me to have a year free and clear to devote to Kipling. As the Andrew Glasgow Writer-in-Residence, Penland School of Crafts, North Carolina, during the summer of 2012, I had a few quiet weeks to develop some early ideas for this book.

I would like to thank my longtime editor, Ann Godoff, and my agent, Melanie Jackson, who believed in this project from the start. I can't imagine a stronger team for a writer. Casey Denis at Penguin Press has been a steady hand along the way.

I have been grateful for the companionship of Kipling scholars, and I wish to thank in particular Alexander Bubb, Sandra Kemp, and Jan Montefiori. Other scholarly debts appear in the Notes section.

Hugh Eakin, former editor of *NYR Daily*, and Professor Montefiori of *The Kipling Journal* gave me space to try out some of the ideas in this book. An early draft of Chapter Eight appeared in *NYR Daily* (July 4, 2015); a discussion of Lockwood Kipling's network of American friends appeared in the May 2018 *Kipling Journal*. I laid out some of the guiding ideas of the book in the December 6, 2013, issue of *The New Republic*, with the encouragement of Leon Wieseltier. It was a particular honor to speak at the "John Lockwood Kipling: Changing Worlds" conference at King's College,

London (March 4, 2017), organized by Professor Bubb and Professor Kemp, and to share the stage with Andrew Lycett and Charles Allen, two Kipling biographers I greatly admire. At an earlier symposium on "Kipling in America: 1892–1896," held at Marlboro College in Vermont in October 2013, I was lucky to spend time with Thomas Penny and Ulrich Knoepflmacher. An early version of Chapter Seven was the Torrence C. Harder Lecture at the Boston Athenaeum, March 14, 2013.

Many friends have helped along the way. A partial list would include Sven Birkerts, Nick Bromell, John Cullen, Joe Ellis, Susan Halpert, Jim Hartley, Megan Marshall, Valerie Martin, Barry Werth, and James Young. Michael Gorra generously read an early draft of the book and made incisive comments. Alex Bubb read the entire book with a shrewd eye for detail. The screenwriter and novelist Bill Nicholson kindly drove me to Bateman's. Neal Rantoul, a terrific photographer and friend, accompanied me to Naulakha for a memorable photo shoot.

My wife, Mickey Rathbun, and our sons, Tommy and Nicholas, have shown the right amount of curiosity and forbearance about each stage of the project. So has my father, who, like Kipling, was a foster child in England, where he first read Kipling. To him I dedicate this book.

NOTES

I have tried to limit this record of sources to the essential. Kipling's writings exist in multiple editions and formats, both British and American; much of his work can also be found online, where it is easily searchable. I have found two selections of Kipling's stories particularly useful: Jan Montefiore, editor, *The Man Who Would Be King: Selected Stories of Rudyard Kipling* (London and New York: Penguin, 2011), and Robert Gottlieb, editor, *Collected Stories* (New York: Everyman, 1994).

Anyone working on Kipling owes a special debt to the painstaking work of Thomas Pinney, who has kindly responded to my queries over the past few years. All poems quoted in this book are from Pinney's authoritative three-volume *The Cambridge Edition of the Poems of Rudyard Kipling* (Cambridge, UK: Cambridge University Press, 2013). Quotations from letters are drawn from Pinney's six-volume edition of *The Letters of Rudyard Kipling* (Iowa City: University of Iowa Press, 1990–2004). While I do not supply references for every letter cited, which would greatly expand this apparatus, interested readers should have no difficulty identifying the approximate date of particular quotations, in those cases where the specific date is not supplied.

Among biographies of Kipling, I have relied primarily on Charles Carrington's *Rudyard Kipling: His Life and Work* (London: Macmillan,

1955) and Andrew Lycett's *Rudyard Kipling* (London: Phoenix, 2000). Pinney's edition of Kipling's autobiography, *Something of Myself and Other Autobiographical Writings* (Cambridge, UK: Cambridge University Press, 1990), notes discrepancies between memory and biographical fact.

The extensive website of the Kipling Society, with its authoritative commentary and generous sampling of Kipling texts—including many of those discussed in this book—is an invaluable resource for anyone interested in Kipling.

Prologue: This Strange Excuse

I am grateful for three pioneering essays on Kipling's engagement with the United States: Thomas Pinney, "Rudyard Kipling and America," William Roger Louis, editor, *Resurgent Adventures with Britannia: Personalities, Politics and Culture in Britain* (London: I. B. Tauris; Austin: Harry Ransom Center, 2011), pp. 31–44; and Judith Plotz, "Kipling's Very Special Relationship: Kipling in America, America in Kipling," in Howard J. Booth, editor, *The Cambridge Companion to Rudyard Kipling* (Cambridge, UK: Cambridge University Press, 2011), pp. 37–51. Simon Schama's remark about Kipling is the opening sentence of his *Landscape and Memory* (1995). Frances Perraudin, "Manchester University Students Paint over Rudyard Kipling Mural," the *Guardian*, July 19, 2018. For Rushdie on Kipling and India, see his introduction to Kipling's *Soldiers Three and In Black and White* (London: Penguin, 1993), p. x. My sense of Kipling's "gravitational pull" during the American Gilded Age is based on such books as Thomas Beer's *The Mauve Decade: American Life at the End of the Nineteenth Century* (1926). George Orwell, "Rudyard Kipling," in *A Collection of Essays by George Orwell* (New York: Anchor, 1954), pp. 127 (on less civilized men protecting civilization) and 133 (on phrases Kipling added to the English language). Auden mentions Kipling in "In Memory of W. B. Yeats." The Borges quotation is in Eliot Weinberger, editor, *Jorge Luis Borges: Selected Non-Fiction* (New York: Penguin, 1999), p. 251.

Chapter One: A Denizen of the Moon

The principal sources for this chapter are Kipling's travel letters from his 1889 journey, collected in the two volumes of *From Sea to Sea* (New York: Doubleday, 1899), and Benjamin Griffin and Harriet Elinor Smith, editors, *Autobiography of*

Mark Twain, vol. 2 (Berkeley and Los Angeles: University of California Press, 2013), pp. 176–77. Kipling's account of his interview with Mark Twain, the final letter in *From Sea to Sea*, is available online: http://storyoftheweek.loa.org/2010/04/interview-with-mark-twain.html.

Chapter Two: At Longfellow's Grave

I wish to thank Alexander Bubb for suggesting to me, in conversation, the possible importance of Kipling's visit to Longfellow's grave, and for his treatment of Kipling and spiritualism in his book *Meeting Without Knowing It: Kipling and Yeats at the Fin de Siècle* (Oxford, UK: Oxford, University Press, 2016). Carrington cites a letter from de Forest (p. 132) on the encounter between Kipling and Henry Harper. On William James and the American Society for Psychical Research, I have relied on Deborah Blum's *Ghost Hunters: William James and the Search for the Scientific Proof of Life After Death* (New York: Penguin Press, 2006). Janet Oppenheim's *The Other World: Spiritualism and Psychical Research in England, 1850–1914* (Cambridge, UK: Cambridge University Press, 1985) gives the English side of the story, with conclusions about the "cross correspondences" on p. 134. Kipling mentions Myers's *Phantasms of the Living* in "The Dreitarbund" (1887). A. W. Baldwin, in *The Macdonald Sisters* (London: Peter Davis, 1960), quotes Kipling on the perils of spiritualism (p. 126). Gerald Balfour, brother of Prime Minister Arthur Balfour, described one of the cases of "cross correspondences" in his book *The Ear of Dionysius: Farther Scripts Affording Evidence of Personal Survival* (New York: Henry Holt, 1920). William Dillingham, in the first chapter of *Rudyard Kipling: Life, Love, and Art* (Greensboro, North Carolina: ELT Press, 2013), argues that Charlie is a con man. Borges translated Kipling's story; Brecht adapted a German translation of "Song of the Galley Slave" and published it under his own name; Eliot particularly admired the poem. James K. Lyon, "Brecht's Use of Kipling's Intellectual Property: A New Source of Borrowing," in *Monatshefte*, vol. 61, no. 4 (winter 1969), pp. 376–86.

Chapter Three: A Death in Dresden

For details of Wolcott Balestier's life and career, I have relied primarily on Lycett's account, pp. 296–317. Balestier's *James G. Blaine: A Sketch of His Life* was published by R. Worthington in 1884. Henry James's tribute to Balestier is included in *The American Essays of Henry James*, edited by Leon Edel (New York: Vintage, 1956). Edmund Gosse's tribute is in *Portraits and Sketches* (New York: Scribner,

1914). Edel's *Henry James: The Middle Years, 1882–1895* (New York: Avon, 1978) has a nuanced account of James's relationship with Balestier (pp. 282–84, 287–89); Alice James's assessment of Balestier is on p. 299. Fred Kaplan, in *Henry James: The Imagination of Genius* (New York: Morrow, 1992), quotes Balestier's offer to attend James's first play (p. 352). In Willa Cather's novella *Coming, Aphrodite!* the artist Don Hedger resembles Dick Heldar. Lycett quotes Balestier on the progress of *The Naulahka* (p. 311); Carrington quotes Balestier on the division of labor (p. 181). Lycett quotes Carrie's letter to Josephine about their friendship with Kipling (p. 304). The title of the novel, with its misplaced *k*, was mysteriously misspelled; it should have read *The Naulakha*. On the effect of Balestier's death on James, see Edel, *Henry James: The Treacherous Years, 1895–1910* (1969; New York: Avon, 1978), pp. 48–50; on James and Kipling, see pp. 50–59. On Harry Macdonald and his sisters, see Judith Flanders, *A Circle of Sisters: Alice Kipling, Georgiana Burne-Jones, Agnes Poynter, and Louisa Baldwin* (New York: Norton, 2005), p. 230. Lycett quotes Heinemann's concerns about Balestier running their company from the Isle of Wight (p. 317).

Chapter Four: A Buddha Snowman

The primary source for this chapter is *Kipling's Japan: Collected Writings,* edited by Hugh Cortazzi and George Webb (London: Athlone, 1988), especially two travel letters from 1892: "Our Overseas Men" and "Some Earthquakes." Additional material is drawn from chapter 5, "The Committee of Ways and Means," of *Something of Myself.* Kipling's "In Sight of Monadnock" first appeared in the *Springfield [Massachusetts]Republican* (April 17, 1892). Kipling quoted Emerson's "Woodnotes" from memory; the final line should read, "And the ripples in rhymes the oar forsake." Reviewing Kipling's *Letters of Travel* in 1920, Virginia Woolf praised the passage about the ruined "Outside Men," noting how Kipling managed to convey "much more vividly than by means of direct description ... the excitement and strangeness of the East." See "Mr. Kipling's Notebook" in Mary Lyon, editor, *Books and Portraits: Some Further Selections from the Literary and Biographical Writings of Virginia Woolf* (New York: Harcourt Brace, 1978).

Chapter Five: An Ark for Josephine

Kipling's initial impressions of Brattleboro are recorded in chapter 5 of *Something of Myself.* See also Stuart Murray, *Rudyard Kipling in Vermont: Birthplace of the Jungle Books* (Brattleboro, VT: Images from the Past, 1997). Edward Said compares human diversity in *Kim* to a Noah's Ark in his introduction to the novel (New York: Penguin, 1987), p. 42. On the possible connection between Naulakha and Kashmiri house-boats, see Julius Bryant, "Kipling as a Designer," in Julius Bryant and Susan Weber, editors, *John Lockwood Kipling: Arts and Crafts in the Punjab and London* (New York: Bard Graduate Center Gallery; New Haven and London: Yale University Press, 2017), p. 140. It has been assumed, based on a comment by Mary Cabot, that Henry Rutgers Marshall was a friend of the Balestier family, but de Forest seems a more likely inter-mediary. Records of Columbia undergraduate classes are available online. Henry Rutgers Marshall, *Pain, Pleasure, and Aesthetics* (London and New York: Macmillan, 1894), p. 321. William James's (unsigned) review of Marshall's book appeared in *The Nation*, vol. 59 (1894). For details of the Wesselhoeft Water Cure and similar nineteenth-century therapeutic communities, I am grateful to Philip Gura, *Man's Better Angels: Romantic Reformers and the Coming of the Civil War* (Cambridge, MA: Harvard University Press, 2017). For three recent accounts of John Humphrey Noyes, see Chris Jennings, *Paradise Now: The Story of American Utopianism* (New York: Random House, 2016); Erik Reece, *Utopia Drive: A Road Trip Through America's Most Radical Idea* (New York: Farrar, Straus and Giroux, 2018); and Ellen Wayland-Smith, *Oneida: From Free Love Utopia to the Well-Set Table* (New York: Picador, 2016). For visitors to Brattle-boro, see Molly Cabot's *Annals of Brattleboro, 1681–1895* (Brattleboro: E. L. Hildreth, 1921), in two volumes. Conan Doyle's report on his visit to Naulakha is included in Harold Orel, editor, *Kipling: Interviews and Recollections, vol. 2* (Totowa, NJ: Barnes and Noble, 1983), pp. 237-38. Kipling's golf clubs remain at Naulakha. A talk delivered by Professor Ulrich Knoepflmacher at a symposium organized by the Kipling Society and held at Marlboro College, near Brattleboro, on October 7–8, 2013, clarified for me the range of Kipling's use of symbols like Noah's Ark. See Knoepflmacher, "Kipling's American 'Berangements' for the Young," in *The Kipling Journal*, vol. 88, no. 355 (July 2014), pp. 58–74. Three elements of Kipling's life and work—his traumatic experience as an abandoned, foreign-born child, with religiously obsessed foster par-ents in England; the Masonic symbolism of Noah's Ark; and a toy Noah's Ark—reappear in the German-born writer W. G. Sebald's novel *Austerlitz*.

Chapter Six: The Fourth Dimension

The best source on Kipling's father is Bryant and Weber, editors, *John Lockwood Kipling: Arts and Crafts in the Punjab and London*. Sandra Kemp's contribution to the volume, "'An Expert Fellow-Craftsman': Rudyard Kipling and the Pater," explores the personal and professional relationship between father and son. My account of

Kipling's opium use relies on Charles Allen, *Kipling Sahib: India and the Making of Rudyard Kipling* (New York: Pegasus, 2019), pp. 165–74. According to Allen, Kipling's use of drugs "brought a new dimension to his thinking" (p. 171). For Dr. Robert Dawbarn's article "Opium in India—A Medical Interview with Rudyard Kipling," see Harold Orel, editor, *Kipling: Interviews and Recollections*, vol. 1, pp. 108-9. Thomas Pinney includes Kipling's diary of 1885 in his edition of *Something of Myself and Other Biographical Writings*, pp. 195–218. The entry about *"Mother Maturin"* is on p. 207. Lycett quotes Edmonia Hill's account of the novel, p. 140. Kipling's "In an Opium Factory" was included in *From Sea to Sea*. Henry Adams prays to the dynamo in the famous twenty-fifth chapter, "The Dynamo and the Virgin," of *The Education of Henry Adams* (Boston: Houghton Mifflin, 1918). Jorge Luis Borges notes, "The Italian futurists forget that [Kipling] was the first European poet to celebrate the superb and blind activity of machines." See Weinberger, editor, *Borges: Selected Non-Fiction*, p. 251. On Kipling's use of the "vehicles" of the Hindu gods, see Harish Trivedi, "Of Beasts and Gods in India: Lockwood Kipling's *Beast and Man* and Rudyard Kipling's 'The Bridge-Builders,'" in *The Kipling Journal*, vol. 92, no. 373 (May 2018), pp. 38–41.

Chapter Seven: Adopted by Wolves

Kipling published *The Jungle Book* in 1894. He published *The Second Jungle Book* the following year. The two volumes are often combined and referred to as *The Jungle Book* (as in this book) or *The Jungle Books*. On Sir William Henry Sleeman's pamphlet, *An Account of Wolves Nurturing Children in Their Dens* (Plymouth, 1852), as a source for Kipling, see Daniel Karlin's introduction to *The Jungle Books* (London: Penguin, 1987), pp. 14, 16–19. As Karlin notes, "Mowgli is almost the exact inverse of Sleeman's typical wolf-child" (p. 18). For an example of mass hysteria centering on wolf phobia in the South of France, see Jay M. Smith, *Monsters of the Gévaudan: The Making of the Beast* (Cambridge, MA: Harvard University Press, 2011). Smith concludes that the wolf-monster embodied widespread fears of political and religious disruption of village life following the French Revolution. Molly Cabot's short memoir *Kipling in America: 1892–1896* (1911) can be accessed on the Kipling Society website: http://www.kiplingsociety.co.uk/rg_vermont_cabot.htm. Lockwood Kipling's view of America as a good place for independent thinkers is quoted in Bryant and Weber, editors, *John Lockwood Kipling: Arts and Crafts in the Punjab and London*, p. 55. I have made liberal use of Molly Cabot's *Annals of Brattleboro, 1681–1895*. Carrie Kipling's diary was destroyed, but extracts copied by two of Kipling's biographers (Carrington and Lord Birkenhead) are among the documents in the University of Sussex collection, where I found the mention of Mary Wilkins. On the persecution of wolves in the United States, see Barry Lopez, *Of Wolves and Men* (New York: Scribner, 1978); Lopez quotes Roger Williams and Theodore Roosevelt on p. 142. See also Garry Marvin, *Wolf* (London: Reaktion, 2012), who discusses *The Jungle Book* as an example of "lupophilia" on pp. 134–39. Ellen Wayland-Smith, *Oneida*, gives close attention to the community's production of animal traps. On Freud and Kipling, see Peter Gay, *Reading Freud: Explorations and Entertainments* (New Haven: Yale University Press, 1991), pp. 98, 105. I am indebted to a conversation with Ulrich Knoepflmacher for the connection between Kipling's Mowgli and Sendak's Max, in *Where the Wild Things Are.* I share Knoepflmacher's belief that the likely intermediary was the poet-critic Randall Jarrell, a Kipling enthusiast who collaborated with Sendak on several children's books.

Chapter Eight: At the Washington Zoo

The best account of what Henry Adams referred to as the "little Washington gang" is Patricia O'Toole, *The Five of Hearts: An Intimate Portrait of Henry Adams and His Friends, 1880–1918* (New York: Ballantine, 1990). For John Hay's pursuit of Elizabeth Cameron, see John Taliaferro, *All the Great Prizes: The Life of John Hay from Lincoln to Roosevelt* (New York: Simon and Schuster, 2014), pp. 11, 268–70. For the origins of the National Zoological Park in Washington, see the website of the Smithsonian Archives: https://siarchives.si.edu/history/national-zoological-park. For Spring Rice on Kipling at the zoo, see David H. Burton, *Cecil Spring Rice: A Diplomat's Life* (Madison, NJ: Fairleigh Dickinson University Press, 1990), p. 103. On the Boone and Crockett Club, see Jonathan Spiro, *Defending the Master Race: Conservation, Eugenics, and the Legacy of Madison Grant* (Lebanon, NH: University Press of New England, 2009); on the Forest Reserve Act, see pp. 54–55. Kipling's account of the beavers in Yellowstone is in *From Sea to Sea.* On Phillips in Vermont, see Lycett, p. 375. For a brief history of the Teddy Bear, see the National Park Service website for the Theodore Roosevelt birthplace: https://www.nps.gov/thrb/learn/historyculture/storyofteddybear.htm.

Chapter Nine: A Fishing Trip

Richard Watson Gilder describes Grover Cleveland as a fisherman in *Grover Cleveland: A Record of a Friendship* (New York: Century, 1910), pp. 60–62. I rely on

David Gilmour's account of the Venezuela crisis in *The Long Recessional: The Imperial Life of Rudyard Kipling* (New York: Farrar, Straus and Giroux, 2002), pp. 111–13. "The White Seal" was a favorite story of Antonio Gramsci. Richard Hofstadter, in *The American Political Tradition and the Men Who Made It* (1948; New York: Vintage, 1973), quotes Roosevelt on the necessity of a war (on p. 275) and gives his assessment of Cleveland on p. 232. Henry Miller referred to the United States as an "air-conditioned nightmare." On Kipling and Winslow Homer, see Nicolai Cikovsky Jr. and Franklin Kelly, *Winslow Homer* (New Haven: Yale University Press, 1996), pp. 226, 229–30. For details of Kipling's lawsuit against Beatty, I rely on Frederic F. Van De Water, "Rudyard Kipling's Vermont Feud" (1937), reprinted in Harold Orel, editor, *Kipling: Interviews and Recollections, vol. 2*, pp. 220–30. "The Moral Equivalent of War," in Ralph Barton Perry, editor, William James, *Essays on Faith and Morals* (New York: Meridian, 1962), pp. 311–28.

Chapter Ten: Dharma Bums

Jack Kerouac's *The Dharma Bums* aligns its two main protagonists with the legendary Buddhist monks Han Shan and Shih-te (Hanshan and Shide), just as Kipling models Kim and the Teshoo Lama on Ananda and the Buddha. Kipling's memories of the Burne-Jones household and environs, and the origins of *Kim*, are drawn from *Something of Myself* unless otherwise indicated. The best account of Kipling and the Macdonald family is Judith Flanders, *A Circle of Sisters*. Angela Thirkell describes visits with Kipling in *Three Houses* (Oxford: Oxford University Press, 1931). Hannah Arendt's brilliant analysis of *Kim* is in *The Origins of Totalitarianism* (New York: Harcourt, 1985), pp. 216–18. It seems likely that her close friend Randall Jarrell first brought *Kim* to her attention. Borges linked *Kim* and *Huckleberry Finn* in his lecture "The Argentine Writer and Tradition," in Weinberger, editor, *Jorge Luis Borges: Selected Non-Fiction*, p. 424. Mark Twain's travels in India are recorded in *Following the Equator*, in Roy Blount Jr., editor, *Mark Twain: A Tramp Abroad, Following the Equator, Other Travels* (New York: Library of America, 2010), pp. 641–44, 662, 759.

Chapter Eleven: War Fever

For details of the Kipling family in New York, I have drawn on Lycett's account, pp. 419–24. The best account of Kipling's support for American empire is Gilmour, *The Long Recessional*. For historical background, and for the debate about the occupation of the Philippines, see Stephen Kinzer, *The True Flag: Theodore Roosevelt, Mark Twain, and the Birth of American Empire* (New York: Henry Holt, 2017). Kinzer discusses "The White Man's Burden" and the Senate vote (p. 120), Senator Lodge on the Philippines as a market for American goods (p. 41), McKinley's voice from God (p. 87), Hay on the "splendid little war" (p. 58), Roosevelt on San Juan Hill (p. 55), and William James on Roosevelt's praise of war (p. 22). For Roosevelt's letter to Kipling about pirates and headhunters, see Kinzer, p. 12. Kipling's dream diary is included as an appendix, titled "Kipling's Delirium," in Lord Birkenhead, *Rudyard Kipling* (London: Weidenfeld and Nicolson, 1978). Borges compares Kipling and Kafka in a 1946 essay called "Our Poor Individualism," in Weinberger, editor, *Selected Non-Fictions*, p. 310. Gilmour discusses the relationship between "The White Man's Burden" and "Recessional," "two of the most famous poems in the English language," on pp. 119–32. On Kipling's use of Emerson in "Recessional" (a debt first noted by Birkenhead), and the vision of empire extending from Canada to Ceylon, see Gilmour, p. 121. Thirkell describes Kipling after Josephine's death in *Three Houses.* On Josephine's death as inscribed in *Just So Stories,* see U. C. Knoepflmacher, "Kipling's 'Just-So' Partner: The Dead Child as Collaborator and Muse," in *Children's Literature,* vol. 25 (1997), pp. 24–49.

Chapter Twelve: The Flooded Brook

Mark Twain's account of receiving an honorary degree from Oxford is in Benjamin Griffin and Harriet Elinor Smith, editors, *Autobiography of Mark Twain,* vol. 3 (Berkeley and Los Angeles: University of California Press, 2015), pp. 81–84. Some of Kipling's drawings in the margins of his volumes of Horace are reproduced in Sandra Kemp, "'An Expert Fellow-Craftsman,'" in Bryant and Weber, editors, *John Lockwood Kipling,* p. 414. I am grateful to Professor Kemp for conversations at the Victoria and Albert Museum concerning these fascinating drawings, which might be compared to the illuminated manuscripts in Kipling's story "The Eye of Allah." Since Kipling claimed, near the end of his life, that "If—" had been inspired by Jameson's Raid, it is interesting to find Mark Twain, in *Following the Equator,* applying an oddly similar volley of conditionals to Jameson's doomed raid: "If I had been with Jameson the morning after he started, I should have advised him to turn back. That was Monday; it was then that he received his first warning from a Boer source not to violate the friendly soil of the Transvaal. It showed that his invasion was known. If I had been with him on Tuesday morning and afternoon, when he received further warnings, I should have repeated my advice. If I had been with him the next morning—New Year's—when he received notice that 'a few hundred' Boers were waiting for him a few miles ahead, I should not have advised, but commanded him to go back. And if I had been with him two or three hours later—a thing not conceivable to me—I should have retired him by force." Twain comments on Kipling's "South Africa" in *Autobiography of Mark Twain*, vol. 2 (2013), p. 175; see also p. 544 for Twain's comments on Kipling's training and early beliefs. Burne-Jones's advice about the Puck books is quoted in Carrington, p. 376. I first heard "Harp Song of the Dane Women" in Robert Fitzgerald's verse-writing class at Harvard, a memorable occasion. "They" inspired a ghostly passage in T. S. Eliot's "Burnt Norton," the first of the *Four Quartets*, in which the "hidden laughter" of children echoes through a rural garden. Kipling's account of his dream is in the final chapter, "Working-Tools," of *Something of Myself*. Mark Twain's predictive dream about the death of his brother is discussed in Blum, *Ghost Hunters*, p. 73. Film technology is used to uncanny effect in Kipling's story "Mrs. Bathgate."

Epilogue: American Hustle

The topic of Kipling and Vietnam is, as far as I am aware, a new one. This epilogue took shape around Kipling's pervasive presence in Philip Caputo's *A Rumor of War* (New York: Ballantine, 1977). Vietnam is referred to as a "splendid little war" on p. 63; Kipling's Tommy Atkins is invoked on p. xx; Caputo reads Kipling's lines about hustling the East on pp. 92–93. Viet Thanh Nguyen invokes "The White Man's Burden" in *Nothing Ever Died: Vietnam and the Memory of War* (Cambridge, MA: Harvard University Press, 2016), p. 251. "A century later," he writes, the poem "may as well describe my war and its aftermath in our current American wars in the Middle East." In *Dispatches* (New York: Knopf, 1977), Michael Herr refers to those who remember the past on p. 254 and mentions the view that Vietnam would be an easy war on p. 95. For Kipling and the Boy Scouts, see Hugh Brogan, *Mowgli's Sons: Kipling and Baden-Powell's Scouts* (London: Jonathan Cape, 1987). Lycett mentions Kermit Roosevelt's visit at Bateman's and Allen Dulles's fondness for *Kim*, a book that, as Lycett notes, "attained mythical status among American spies" (p. 550). Christian Appy first suggested to me, in conversation, that Edward Lansdale's enthusiasm for Kipling might be worth pursuing. I am grateful for Appy's book *American Reckoning: The Vietnam War and Our National Identity* (New York: Penguin, 2015) for many details (such as Diem's ties to American Catholics) as well as for his overall portrayal of American deception during the war. Lansdale's use of *Kim* is detailed in Richard Drinnon, *Facing West: The Metaphysics of Indian-Hating and Empire-Building*

(Norman, OK: University of Oklahoma Press, 1997), pp. 385–87. It is widely believed that Lansdale served as the model for Graham Greene's Alden Pyle in *The Quiet American* (1955). For Greene, Pyle, with all his schemes and strategies, is another fool who tried to hustle the East. In *The Road Not Taken: Edward Lansdale and the American Tragedy in Vietnam* (New York: Liveright, 2018), Max Boot notes that Greene had written a draft of the novel before Lansdale arrived in Saigon. "Yet the identification of Lansdale as 'the Quiet American' adheres like indelible ink, because the views that Greene ascribes to Alden Pyle are an identifiable caricature of the views held by Lansdale" (p. xliii). My account of the interactions between Harkins and Westmoreland is drawn from Stanley Karnow, *Vietnam: A History* (New York: Penguin, 1997). Karnow quotes Harkins on Kipling (p. 291), mentions Lodge's impatience (p. 267), quotes Dean Rusk (p. 345), quotes Westmoreland on the impending end of the war (p. 779), and raises the question of American deception with regard to the Tet Offensive (p. 543). Mark Twain called the American presence in the Philippines a "quagmire" in "To One Sitting in Darkness" (1901). For John Huston on the contemporary significance of *The Man Who Would Be King*, see Axel Madsen, *John Huston* (New York: Doubleday, 1978), p. 244. Ward Just, a novelist who had covered the Vietnam War as a reporter, criticized the famous scene in *The Deer Hunter* in which an American POW is forced to play Russian roulette while a Vietnamese audience bets on the results. Just called the harrowing scene "a crisp update" of Kipling's line "Here lies a fool who tried to hustle the East." See Steven Biel, "The *Deer Hunter* Debate: Artistic License and Vietnam War Remembrance," in *Bright Lights Film Journal* (July 25, 2016) at brightlightsfilm.com online.

INDEX

Page numbers in *italics* refer to illustrations.